JULIUS WEITMANN

PORSCHE
STORY

English language version by
Charles Meisl

arco **ARCO PUBLISHING COMPANY, INC.**
NEW YORK

Published by ARCO PUBLISHING COMPANY, INC.
219 Park Avenue South, New York, N.Y. 1003

© 1967 mvg, Moderne Verlags-GmbH, Munchen 23
© 1968 Patrick Stephens Limited

Library of Congress Catalog Card Number 69-11868

ARCO Catalog Number 668-01843-7

Printed in Great Britain

Foreword

THE IDEA FOR this book goes back a few years. It only took concrete shape because of a good-neighbour relationship with Porsche, (my house is only a few miles from the Zuffenhausen works), which led to my having the necessary confidence required to produce a great number of unique pictorial documents.

Our thanks are therefore due to those who, despite our off-beat wishes, never tired of giving advice and help. This picture series does not by any means claim completeness, yet it is the expression of our immense love and esteem for a motor car, which today has found its enthusiasts in every corner of the globe.

It is to those that this book is dedicated. It is trying to convey to them the reason for spending 18 years pursuing everything connected with the name Porsche, way beyond professional interest. It is by way of a tribute to a handful of men who, on alien soil and starting with nothing apart from unbelievable idealism, began to work without knowing where their way would lead, and with one goal only—to create something after all had sunk to dust and ruins.

It is gratifying to us that many of these men are still alive and can therefore participate in this review of the past, where their contributions have merited unstinted praise. The chronicler, who for half a lifetime has "written" with a camera almost exclusively in the world of the motor car, following its design in the experimental department through his viewfinder, or its disappearance from the edge of the racing circuit, and who has known the shattering hopelessness of an open grave, becomes critical of himself and his surroundings. So here is a word of excuse to those who might think some of the pictures too awkward: fractions of seconds have sometimes decided many of these photographs.

This then is a flashback showing the pride and the pleasure, and also the bitterness and the disappointment. Neither one nor the other should remain hidden. To understand and appreciate fully what we wanted to communicate here requires the ability of sharing, alone and far from home, the emotions which can be released by victory and defeat.

However very often a picture speaks louder than words, and we hope that this is the case in some of these pictures.

Julius J. Wietmann
Stuttgart-Botnang

Foreword to the U.S. edition

MOTORING ENTHUSIASM has been ingrained in Julius Weitmann since boyhood, and his enthusiasm shines through this delightful pictorial survey—the result of 18 years of pointing his camera at all Porsche happenings wherever they occurred. He has also recorded the Continental motoring scene freelance-fashion for the picture magazines and automobile publications of Germany and elsewhere.

A certain nostalgia pervades these pages—particularly those featuring many of the protagonists of this splendid sport who, alas, are no longer with us.

I am delighted to be associated with this English language version, for I drove the first Porsche in England in 1951 and subsequently was responsible for the appearance of the first three cars in that country.

Charles Meisl

London, August 1968

The Years of Porsche

N MARCH 21 1951 work stopped at Porsche's for hour to mark the production of the 500th car. (The st was finished at Easter 1950.) At that time, the hall labour force were in effect "lodging" in the ighbouring Reutter coachworks and only used 500 uare metres (some 5,400 square feet) of working area, ased to the company at one Deutschmark per square etre. Twenty metres housed the production manager, ages office and the research and personnel manager, ans Klauser, (seated in car), who is Service Manager day, while the management and design office were housed in a pre-fab which had been purchased for 19,000 Deutschmarks (about £1,580 at that time) and covered about 100 square metres (some 1,080 square feet). In 1949, Klauser had hired the first workman, Herbert Linge, who is today principal foreman. At the furthest left is Karl Kirn, trustee from 1949–51. Today he is Manager and Chief of Purchasing. This 1,100 cc 40 bhp Porsche sold at 9,950 Deutschmarks (about £830 then). The 1,000th car was finished on August 28 1951, and the 5,000th on March 15 1954.

THE TIME OF THE GREAT Porsche successes had begun. Everywhere in Europe they were winning on circuits, in long-distance races or in rallies. In 1954, Herrmann, von Frankenberg, Polensky and von Hanstein, (pictured, right), took the first four places in the GP of Europe at the Nürburgring. Every weekend the sports columns mentioned the Porsche drivers, Trenkel, Götze, Engel, Count Einsiedel, Ringgenberg, Heuberger, Mathé, Glöckler, Seidel, Rolff, Strähle, Greger, Nathan, von Trips, Storez, etc.

From 1952, Porsche and Daimler-Benz jointly represented Germany's colours again. On the southern Swedish circuit of Kristianstad—the smallest and narrowest imaginable—the 1955 gull-wing 300 SL Mercedes were driven by Karl Kling and Count Wolfgang Berghe von Trips (former Porsche driver), in the same class as the Porsche Spyders. Paul Frère (no 22) in the Ferrari (below) led at first, but neither he nor the "C" type Jaguar, (Kurt Lincoln from Finland), stayed the distance. The winner was von Frankenberg in the 1,500 cc Porsche Spyder (no 25).

THE 1,000 MILES of Brescia (Mille Miglia) was, apart from the Targa Florio, the biggest and most important road race in the world and it meant an important victory for Porsche in 1955. The start and finish was in Brescia, where the cars started during the night at two-minute intervals. Glöckler/Seidel in the Spyder 550 had the number 541: that is to say the car started at 05.41 hours. They won their class and were 8th overall among cars of twice their engine size. Their time for the 1,600 kilometres was 12 hrs 8 mins 17 secs, and they are pictured (bottom left) on the Raticosa pass.

R. von Frankenberg/Count Oberndorff in the 1300 S Coupé (no 244) defeated the Alfa Romeos in the 1300 class, and R. Günzler won the 1600 GT class with his Porsche.

Two years later the Mille Miglia was held for the last time in its classic form. The Italian Government prohibited it after the Spaniard, Marquis de Portago, and several spectators were killed in an accident. For many years it constituted a spring festival, and millions of Italians enthusiastically participated in it. It would have become indefensible in the long run, however, as some cars reached 180 mph and there was absolutely no protection for the spectators.

In the all-German Avus race of 1955, the EMW's from Eisenach, driven by Barth, Rosenhammer, Thiel and Binner, tried all they knew to beat von Frankenberg's leading Spyder. Barth did not finish, and Rosenhammer was placed second. The centre picture shows the winner on the north curve of the Avus.

THEY CALLED this airfreight jo[...] "Operation Caracas" when a 150[...] Spyder was flown for the first time t[...] the Sportscar Grand Prix of Caraca[...] In a powerful field of Ferrari[...] Maseratis and Gordinis, von Hanstei[...] managed 8th place. A little late[...] Porsche chalked up one of their mo[...] resounding victories at Le Man[...] Gregor Grant, writing in Autospor[...] referred to them as "these incredibl[...] cars", when five of the six that ha[...] started finished 24 hours later i[...] excellent positions. Polensky/vo[...] Frankenberg, (shown below at th[...] wheel), won the important Index c[...] Performance with their 1,500 c[...] vehicle.

The German races were noteworth[...] for their fierce but fair contests. I[...] this 500 kilometre event on th[...] Nürburgring series production, G[...] and special touring cars compet[...] happily together (right).

1956

THE 25TH BIRTHDAY of the Porsche company coincided with the completion of the 10,000th type 356 in the spring of 1956. Our pictures show the assembly hall of No 2 works, in which 650 people were by now employed, and it is only a few yards to the Reutter coachworks which today belong to Porsche.

The "Jubilee" car was conceived, designed and tested in the No 1 works, birthplace of the Volkswagen and for a long time used by the occupation forces, afterwards as Stuttgart's typhoid hospital. After the festivities were over, the youngest driver of the Porsche family, Wolfi,—Ferry Porsche's youngest son—drove it out of the works. Among the guests of honour we see from right to left: Mrs Porsche (the widow of the great designer), today's Boss, Ferry, (Wolfi between them,) and Mrs Louise Piëch, Ferry's sister and part-owner of the company since 1938, who looked after the firm in the tough post-war years whilst the management was interned. Next to her is Stuttgart's Mayor, Dr Arnulf Klett.

AS IN ALL the years before and after, in 1956 the Porsches again had their temporary "home" for the "Vingt Quatre Heures du Mans" in a small garage at Teloché, about eight miles from the circuit, (left upper picture). Porsche's hopes were concentrated entirely on von Trips/von Frankenberg (no 25) after Herrmann had dropped out because of engine trouble. Could that pair of drivers continue the series of past class victories! Their 1500 RS Spyder had a hardtop and a flat, curved tail; it did not show any signs of the manx-like cut-off rear end which became such common wear in later years. If things proceeded to plan, then refuelling and driver changes coincided every three hours. Fuel capacity of those cars was between 20 and 22 gallons (imp).

The top picture shows Hild, the racing engineer, refuelling—a somewhat dicey job! He is checked by two officials, one of whom is responsible for the sealing of the fuel tank. No 25 won its class, finished a high 5th in the general classification and 2nd in the Index of Performance, covering 3,792 kilometres, (about 2,354 miles).

THIS IS HOW we saw th
opening lap of the sports ca
racing event that preceded th
Formula 1 German Grand Prix
Here, at the lowest point of th
"Fuchsröhre", the positions are
Roy Salvadori (Cooper-Clima
no 37) first, then Hans Herrman
(51) and Wolfgang von Trip
(52) in their Spyders. No 56 i
Edgar Barth—at the time he wa
top driver for EMW of Easter
Germany—then after a small ga
the two Porsche Spyders c
Umberto Maglioli (54) an
Richard von Frankenberg (53
Later on this first lap, von Trip
overtook not only Salvado
but also Herrmann (at th
"Bergwerk"), but overtaxed h
engine and retired at the end c
the lap. Herrmann also passe
Salvadori and led the field, the
Stirling Moss came through in
new 1500 Maserati after havin
made a poor start. Nevertheles
Herrmann won with a three
second lead. After Salvado
came von Frankenberg an
Maglioli in 4th and 5th position
Of the four EMWs three re
tired with back axle troubles.

PORSCHE ACES Umberto Maglioli (bottom right) and Wolfgang Count Berghe von Trips (bottom left). After both drivers scored splendid class victories at the 1000 Kilometres on the "Ring", Maglioli notched up the—until then—most resounding Porsche win, at the Targa Florio in Sicily. Driving alone, he managed the 720 kilometres (446 miles) in 7 hrs 54 mins 22 secs against the twice-as-powerful Ferraris, Maseratis and Mercedes! At the end, he got out of his Spyder as stiff as a board and could barely move his sunburnt arms. He is one of the last "gentleman drivers" and still successful today. The top picture shows von Trips during the 1000 Kilometres at the "Brünnchen" right hander on the Nürburgring. (A map on Page 139 shows the relevant points of the circuit.)

RIGHT: THE LEADER of this 1,00
Kilometres race, Eugenio Castellotti in his 3
Ferrari, only managed to pass Maglioli
Spyder after 24 laps. What seemed impossib
actually did happen—Umberto kept 20–3
yards behind that very superior machine ov
a distance of three laps, although losing secon
gear right at the beginning.

The top left picture shows Maglioli in th
Junek curve after the Breidscheider bridg
Below is shown the exhaust system and th
new double universal jointed rear axle of th
RS Spyder. Right at the bottom is show
the aerofoil design of the young Swiss engine
and private Spyder owner Michel May.
forecasts the Chaparral spoiler, but the racin
management found the car unacceptable; i
purpose was to ensure better rear whe
adhesion.

On the right: during a GT event at th
Nürburgring, Blendl (Munich) and Zic
(Hannover) battle for the lead in the 1,600 c
class.

THE "SHARK'S MOUTH" car (no 419)—its cockpit is shown top right—was destined for von Hanstein's "secret weapon" Hans Herrmann. Here he is (top left) with his discoverer Erwin Bauer, when they won the 1,500 cc class in the 20th Mille Miglia. The car soon dropped out, however, and Herrmann was not too sorry about this, for it was the race that went down in history as the "rain Mille Miglia" and open cars like Knoch's Spyder (426) "collected" up to four gallons of rainwater! The other centre picture (top) shows D. Lissmann, third in the up to 1,600 cc GT class, after Persson and Nathan, also on Porsches. These two shots were taken on the Raticosa pass at 2 pm, one after the other. At the same time during the previous year there was burning sunshine! Those who have never seen that great classic, the Mille Miglia, have most certainly missed the major motoring event of the century; it was Italy's biggest public festivity with 2–3 million spectators lining its 1,600 kilometres (1,000 miles). The picture at the bottom right shows the cars rushing through Ferrara at night.

O-ONE HAS EVER counted the dark red paving
ones on the banked north curve of the Avus, but all
ose who have raced there know its dangers.

  All that we know of the sensational accident to von
ankenberg on September 16 1956—it was im-
ediately labelled "the miracle of the Avus"—stems
om eye witnesses. von Frankenberg could not tell us
en, nor indeed now—he still has no memory of what
curred. His car, a modified Spyder RS 1500, nick-
amed "Mickey Mouse" led that of von Trips by some
yards, both running above the white line. From
ur position on the Mercedes Tower we saw the car
oming fast into the north curve, then—seemingly
ithout reason—it slewed to the right towards the lip
the banking, shot vertically into the air and turned
ver several times, (see top picture). A detailed en-
rgement, (bottom), shows the instant when von
ankenberg was thrown out of the revolving car.

FRACTIONS OF SECONDS later, the driver's fall was broken by the acacia bushes which grow at the rear of the banking, whilst the car dropped into the pits area. The two centre top pictures show that some of the people there had not yet even noticed what had happened, whilst some others came running with fire extinguishers to save von Frankenberg. No-one knew at that moment that he was not in the car. All efforts to save the wreck, now burning with poisonous white magnesium flames, were in vain. Suddenly, in the midst of this commotion, someone bellowed: "Here he is!"—and they found him hanging from an acacia bush. The photo of the tyre (top right) next to the lip of the banking with the tracks of the slewing car, shows clearly that the racing tyres were pressing against the bodywork. Apart from this, the front of the car is unquestionably different from that of the series-built Spyders (top left).

The GT class also produced interesting battles among the Carrera drivers (left). Behind the unchallenged winner Hammerlund, from Sweden, came Max Nathan, who is seen here a nose in front of Rolf Götze.

THE EXPECTED DUEL between the East German EMWs from Eisenach and the Porsches took place on the latter's home-circuit—Solitude—in July of that year, and more than 300,000 spectators witnessed it. The celebrated local-boy-makes-good, Herrmann, here demonstrates (top right) his smooth style in the "shadow" curve (10), and none of his fellow-competitors came anywhere near. By the way, car no 11 is the very "Mickey Mouse" later destroyed at the Avus in Berlin (see page 29), and also driven here by Richard von Frankenberg. No 7 is a Borgward, driven by Herbert Schulze from Bremen. His car is so far on the outside of the bend that it was impossible, despite shooting from the same position, to get the inner edge of the bend into the camera frame. His victory put Herrmann, with 15.5 points, into the lead for the German championship, ahead of von Trips with 14, and von Frankenberg with 9.5. The picture above shows the same bend further on. In this group of three cars, no 30 is driven by the unforgettable Max Nathan and it was the yellow and blue Spyder belonging to his Swedish friend, Gert Kaiser. This section of the circuit is one of the most popular parts for the spectators, because the cars are not travelling so fast here, having to be braked hard after being on full chat on the only existing straight.

"PORSCHE BEATS the Munich-Rome Express by seven hours". This was the 1951 headline, describing a drive by Richard von Frankenberg and Julius Weitmann in the very first 1300 car that Porsche had produced at the time.

The burning vehicle shown above was this same car which later unfortunately crashed during the Stuttgart aerodrome races when it left the road, having to miss a carelessly overtaking car. It collided with the bank of an underpass and was burnt out. Its driver, Rolf Wütherich, escaped unharmed; he had become well known as James Dean's mechanic before Dean was killed driving in California on September 30 1955.

1957

BEFORE THE Formula I Grand Prix of Germany they ran for the first time a separate race for Formula 2, (up to 1,500 c) cars, wherein Edgar Barth, who had recently joined Porsche's from the Eastern Zone, drove a modified Spyder RS transformed into a racing car (no 21). For ten laps he battled hard with Roy Salvadori in Cooper, (top of the picture, left). These two gave such a show of competence and courage that their race became one of the most exciting of recent years. Great was the spectators' disappointment when the Cooper's right rear wishbone broke, here at the "Brünnchen" descent. In Centro Sud's two-year-old Maserati (17) we saw Hans Herrmann, but the age of the car made it a poor also-ran.

The five times World Champion Juan Manuel Fangio drove the race of his life in a Maserati, and from an almost hopeless position overcame the two leading Ferraris driven by Mike Hawthorn and Peter Collins. Prior to this memorable event, von Hanstein wanted to know accurately just how a five-fold champion would conduct a Porsche round the Ring; whilst Fangio is in the process of getting out, racing manager von Diergardt looks enviously at the smiling Hanstein (top right).

The new year also brought a very much overdue novelty: a fast transporter for two Spyders, which could be quickly loaded and unloaded (right).

THERE HAD hardly ever been such disappointed faces at the "1,000 Kilometres" on the Ring as there were in 1957. First-rate drivers such as Ivor Bueb, Jack Fairman, Ron Flockhart and Ninian Sanderson with their 290 bhp 'D' type Jaguars gave their all for Ecurie Ecosse to keep in front of the half-as-powerful RS Spyders. But the Jaguar's roadholding simply did not suffice, and they were caught and over-taken, such as here (left) by von Frankenberg (22) after the bridge at Breidscheid, the lowest point of the circuit.

During practice, knowledgeable spectators were able to observe the East Zone driver Arthur Rosenhammer in a works Spyder. Rosen-hammer had become the No 1 driver in the EMW Team following Edgar Barth's escape, but he was considerably slower than Barth, (top picture), and thus unable to make use of the chance he was given.

PAIRING Barth with Maglioli for this race was indeed a good move. They set up a new record of 128.8 kph (approximately 80.1 mph) as opposed to 125.5 kph in the previous year. Here we see Maglioli (above) on the steep part of the "Ex Mühle".

With his splendidly prepared and entirely privately owned 1600 GT, Paul Ernst Straehle (a successful VW and Porsche dealer from Schorndo᷅ made sure of the first of his five class wins on t 'Ring (below). He co-drove his "V2" with Pa᷅ Denk who, as a VW test driver, had covered seve᷅ tens of thousands of laps of the 'Ring. Later he c᷅ drove with H. Walter and G. Koch. Shown right a "typically Nürburgring" shot of the field.

THE 24 HOURS of Le Mans were remarkable for the seasonal heat—and for a series of accidents to the Porsches. Although the race had begun well—here (below) is Claude Storez coming into the "Esses", followed by the huge and vastly powerful Maserati driven by Stirling Moss—the night witnessed the retirement of four of the six cars that had started. Storez from France, whilst lying 5th overall, stopped on the circuit out of fuel; for an hour he pushed his car to the pits, forgetting that the regulations necessitated the last lap to be covered in a maximum of 30 minutes. Apart from this, there was an accident just after midnight between Brooks and Maglioli, which fortunately ended well (right). Brooks slid into a sand-bank, was thrown from his Aston Martin and lay senseless next to it on the road. Seconds later Maglioli roared up to the spot and cleverly avoided a collision, but for him also the race was run.

HERE WE HAVE father and son and their latest product, the Spyder with the fins, flat out on the Mulsanne straight a day before the race. Young "Butzi" Porsche lies on the ground (left), filming the car's attitude on the undulating road. Porsche always attached considerable emphasis on good placings in this, one of the most important sports car races; hardly any other event influences sales as much as this French "classic."

Without the class win of private entrants, Hugus (USA) and de Beaufort (Holland), the Porsche disaster would have been complete and no Porsche would have finished after such a promising beginning.

The finned Spyder driven by Barth and Maglioli led by a considerable distance until its tragic end. Porsche had been so used to winning, but now for the first time the question arose: lacking a new engine design, where was the limit of the four cylinder sent to the races every year with more and more horsepower? Years ago, after the event, one would have been able to race for yet another 24 hours, but now one could observe the engine specialists listening worriedly to the engine note after only 12 or 14 hours.

Our pictures underline this point, for the top drivers were now mere spectators. The left-hand one shows father and son Porsche, (the latter seated), then Hans Herrmann, who had come along with the pop singer Bibi Johns, next to the Italian Umberto Maglioli. Next, with umbrella, is Hans Klenk of Continental Tyres, with his wife, talking to von Hanstein (back to camera) and Edgar Barth. The lower right picture shows a driver change between Ed Crawford (USA) and Claude Storez, the pair who were in the race until the end, but were then disqualified.

THE 12 HOURS is to Rheims what the 24 Hours is to Le Mans and this race, which starts at midnight on the triangular high-speed Gueux circuit outside the gates of the champagne town of Rheims, acts like a magnet on motoring enthusiasts. Even for the "old hands" the electrifying atmosphere of the midnight start is an ever-new sensation. At exactly 12 o'clock the Le Mans-type start requires the drivers to run to their cars, parked peacefully outside the pits, start the engines, switch on their powerful lights and, amidst a skelter of spinning wheels and roaring engines, somehow thread their way on to the circuit, to be swallowed seconds later by the giant maw of the Dunlop bridge. Where a few moments ago a French military band marched in company with the flags of many nations, and engine noise made all verbal communication impossible, there is now a few minutes frightening quiet until suddenly the bright-eyed phantoms come roaring along the straight from Thillois past the packed grandstands. And where, 12 hours later, everyone will seek even the tiniest spot of shade to escape the pitiless sun, now the officials and spectators huddle in coats and blankets, beating their arms and stamping their tired feet to restore circulation, since even the summer nights can be very cold among the flat expanse of the wheatfields, for here grows grain, not grapes.

Eleven hours later the two Carrera coupés were lapping regularly, 2 mph faster than the Spyders in 1954. No 48 and 50 (Storez/ Bonnier and Barth/von Frankenberg) finished "ex aequo" in 6th and 7th positions in the general classification after the Ferraris.

NO RACE was as exciti
for so many people as t
Mille Miglia, and he
(above) is the scrutineeri
at Brescia. This was t
24th and last of the
classic and unique rac
Porsche only fielded o
works car—a 1956 Spyd
with Maglioli at the whe
—which finished fifth
the general classificatic
the best-ever placing f
Porsche in this event. T
other Porsche drivers r
privately-entered cars, a
here (left) is no 225, P.
Straehle, who with I
Linge managed an avera
speed of 131 kph (81
mph) and thus won t
1600 GT class.

ON LAND, water and in the air Porsche built up its reputation. First there were 25 cross-country vehicles for the German Army. These amphibious 50 bhp cars (below) were of monocoque construction, had a 4-speed synchromesh gearbox plus an extra synchronised crawler gear, and 4-wheel drive, though the front wheel drive could be disconnected. They also had a 65 per cent climbing ability. Then there were 40 all-purpose aircraft, type RW3, for training, with a

pusher airscrew and powered by a 75 bhp Porsche engine. In 1960/61 Porsche-Diesel tractor production was at its peak and 150,000 were built (bottom). Then the American Gyrodyne company built the type 702 with a 72 bhp engine powering a one-man helicopter (top) with contra-rotating blades, one hundred of which were sold.

1958

48

AN IDEA by the Württemberg Porsche Club soon became known as the "judges' and public prosecutors' run". Good drivers of the club took these public servants out in their cars and demonstrated that driving fast did not necessarily constitute a punishable offence. Due to the constantly increasing traffic density, these runs helped the court's judgment to become somewhat more adapted to modern times. During one of these runs the police chief of Stuttgart stated that he welcomed them, since the civil servants should not be in the position where they did not see the wood for the trees. Since those early days these runs have become regular events each year.

The white police Porsches with their 2-way radios have been in use in four countries for some time now (far left and below).

DESPITE good weather, the fourth 1,000 kilometres race on the Nürburgring attracted only a few spectators, as can be seen here on the very popular "Flugplatz" section (far left).

Porsche had taken on two Grand Prix drivers: Jean Behra, who with Edgar Barth drove the "finned" Spyder, and Harry Schell who was paired off with Paul Frère. They also had the Italian ex-Ferrari driver Scarlatti who left the road during practice at the beginning of the "Fuchsröhre" (left). Borgward's participation for the first time ended in a complete debacle. The cars from Bremen broke down one after the other, for example Jo Bonnier's car, here (below) being passed by von Frankenberg (22). Jean Behra (20) is pictured bottom left about to enter the curve before the "Wehrseifenbrücke," but he was unlucky, suffering a broken valve. The trio von Frankenberg/Barth/de Beaufort managed sixth in the general classification and won their class (centre bottom). The picture bottom right shows Harry Schell at the "Schwalbenschwanz".

HIS YEAR, Porsche's
Mans wishes were ful-
led: sunshine at first,
en a thunderstorm with
tropical downpour and,
five cars that started,
ur finished in third,
urth, fifth and ninth
aces. Even so, how
ould they have fared if
hadn't rained? The class
inners Jean Behra
ottom left) and Hans
errmann covered 3,909.6
lometres (approx 2,427
iles). Top right are
own Ferry Porsche, von
anstein and von Rücker
the pits, and below
em Paul Frère tries to
e under his vizor and
ove the windscreen.

AN HOUR BEFORE the sta
and the flag parade has just star
(top). The sky is darkening a
from the Atlantic Ocean there co
heavy, low clouds boding no goo
Umbrellas and raincoats are bei
brought out and the faces of
mechanics from Zuffenhau
cheer up, for they have reduced
compression ratios from 9.8:1
9.4. This year it just has to work
and last year's defeat must
eradicated. Twenty hours later
can see it in their faces (left): Je
Behra with von Hanstein, w

nkenberg with E. Barth, and
hind them the engine and gear-
x specialists E. Storz (standing)
d T. Huber. Two days earlier in
e workshops (above) of Teloché
lage no-one was to know that
s 29 (foreground), 31 and 32
uld finish in line astern, whilst of
enty-one British cars at the start
ly three would survive the 24
urs. Bottom right is shown two
shaped tubes fixed to a wooden
nk, by which means the engine
mpartment pressures were
asured.

THE DEBUT of the centre-seater car, driven by Jean Behra (above), became a Porsche success way beyond Rheims, for this Formula 2 event prior to the French Grand Prix mustered all the known names in motor racing. Peter Collins with the new 6 cylinder Ferrari managed to pull out a few yards lead at the start against Behra (left) whose win was clear cut. Yet this single-seater was by no means a new car—simply a normal 1500 RSK with central steering and seating and 164 bhp—and it triumphed over 14 Coopers, three Lotuses, three Oscas and the 6 cylinder Ferrari, driven by such stars as Stirling Moss, Collins, Graham Hill, Maurice Trintignant, Roy Salvadori and Cabianca. Below: A driver change during the previous 12-hour race, when Storez/von Frankenberg won the up-to-2,000 cc class.

J.Behra

W. v. Trips

THE EUROPEAN HILLCLIMB CHAMPIONSHIP, which was revived in 1957, was enthusiastically received by the drivers, manufacturers and last, but not least, by the spectators. At Mont Ventoux in Southern France, Schauinsland near Freiburg in Germany, Gaisberg in Austria, Monte Bondone in Italy and the Parnassus in Greece—everywhere they battled for fractions of seconds. In 1958 Porsche won the championship for the first time with von Trips (left in the top right picture). Behra also drove for Porsche (right in the same picture, next to von Hanstein and Hild, the racing engineer). Borgward were the toughest opponents and the Bremen works had engaged excellent drivers like Hans Herrmann and Jo Bonnier (middle and lower pictures on right), who show how the steering wheel is held when taking a sharp right-hander. Below is shown a shoal of sports and GT cars after an early morning practice run at Gaisberg, high above Salzburg.

AIRFIELD RACES are mostly a lot of fun, for nothing too serious usually happens there, but this race at Zeltweg two days after von Trips won the hill climb championship also had, apart from a very international entry, a drama all its own. There was a very exciting background to the 35-lap duel between Jean Behra and von Trips, where the two contestants were never more than 50 yards apart. Behra stated at Gaisberg that Trips' car was faster—therefore they had swapped cars here for, said Jeannot, "to win with such a quick car isn't so difficult". Despite taking chances, the Frenchman lost and Wolfgang had the satisfaction of proving him wrong. Here is Behra (112) usually a nose ahead, at one of the two hairpins.

Below: The start of the GT class up to 1,600 cc, against the splendid mountain backdrop of the Salzkammergut, with three old rivals battling it out. The eventual winner von Frankenberg is in the lead, with Günther on the right and S. Greger on the left.

1959

LEFT: Ferry Porsche on his 50th birthday. Since January 30, 1951, the day his father died, the management of the small but famous works whose products are known the world over had been in his hands. Ferdinand, known as "Ferry" everywhere, was good enough to pose on September 19, 1959, his fiftieth birthday, in front of his youngest "child". Three of his four sons work at Porsche to continue the tradition.

Skill and quality to perfection characterized the products of the Swabian coachworks Reutter in Zuffenhausen (below) where Porsche, coming from his emergency quarters at Gmünd in Carinthia, found a niche until the new works were built and the old ones returned to him.

IN 1950, in these cramped quarters, panelbeaters and assemblers worked side by side and managed to produce 25 cars per month, mostly working by hand for money was short and needed for items other than expensive tools. Tinning with liquid solder and spatula, which nowadays is only seen occasionally when expensive cars are built, was here an everyday practice in bodybuilding. Particular care was devoted to the engine assembly. Each engine was the work of one mechanic who stamped his initials on the engine block with a special punch and who was thus always responsible for that particular engine. Even today—18 years later—some of these specialists still work there, albeit in promoted positions. In 1959 Reutter built 25 bodies a month (25 a day today) and Porsche paid some 5,000 marks each for them (about £420 then). With a little electric transporter each body had to be taken to the assembly line, some 160 yards away, and in 1963 Porsche took over Reutter.

HERE WAS heavy cloud over the "Ring" for this
ɔoo kilometre event and yet again—as often before
-Stirling Moss was half way through the south loop
his green Aston Martin, whilst the rest of the field,
d by Hans Herrmann (see next page), entered it.
emarkable also was the position of H. Linge (24)
ho, with his 1600 GT, lay sixth, but later was unable
finish. He was partnered by the Sicilian baron
icci. Herrmann/Maglioli, however, finished fourth
overall and shared the honours of the day with Moss.
De Beaufort, paired with Edgar Barth, had over-
revved his engine just like the Belgian Goethals (top
picture) whose maximum reading needle showed
9,000 rpm. Carrol Shelby (later to construct the
Cobra car) was there also (below), but remained unplaced with his co-driver Seidel, although Porsche
won the 1600 GT class.

THE PACK is unleashed! The fifth 1,000 Kilometres race at the Nürburgring is barely a few seconds old.

FOUR YEARS after the disappearance of the Mercedes "Silver Arrows" 1959 saw the hoped-for Porsche Grand Prix participation at the town circuit of Monte Carlo. Although it was a total disappointment, because von Trips "parked" the car on the second lap, the decision taken by the works was maintained. Bottom left: First tests of the car at Nürburgring with von Trips, Klaus von Rücker and Wilhelm Hild. Jean Behra—lacking a contract with an important team — built his Behra-Porsche (here, right with Toni Sailer in the driving seat at the Avus in Berlin). Last but not least, Borgward built some fast 1.5 litre engines that

were fitted into Coopers and these became a serious threat to the Zuffenhausen machines. Both vehicles put their stamp on the Formula 2 race at Rheims. It was boiling hot when the field disappeared under the Dunlop bridge (below). Next to the three Cooper-Borgwards were three Porsches at the start—a new single-seater with Jo Bonnier and two central-seater cars driven by von Trips and Colin Davis. Since there wasn't a car for Herrmann, Behra loaned him his own (left). Apart from the German cars, there was a Ferrari, and several Cooper-Climaxes and Lotuses, but none of the foreign cars stood a chance.

THIS FORMULA 2 race at Rheims has made history as one of the most exciting races in motoring sport. Its heroes were Moss and Herrmann. The latter held the lead for several laps, (top) but then lost the race by 12 seconds. Our photo shows the cars on full chat past the pits, way out in front of the rest of the field, their speed exceeding 240 kph (149 mph). The overall distance was 207 kilometres (128 miles) and Moss's Borgward, with fuel injection, won at an average of 118.68 mph. No 10 is the type of car with which he won the race. The monoposto, no 44, in which Bonnier stares at his rev counter, is in the process of overtaking Cliff Allison in the Ferrari, who is adjusting his goggles. Bonnier was third, one minute behind the winner.

HERE WERE 23 runners in this
ormula 2 race at Rheims. The flat,
rodynamically successful central-
ater car is here compared to the
ther clumsy looking single-seater.
conomy of space in a search for
e smallest possible frontal area
as then still a future development,
though Colin Chapman's Lotus
ready pointed the way. Three
ars were to pass before the
cision was taken to design a
w, efficient and also beautiful
dy shape to conform to the
quirements of the day.

AS ALWAYS in the Dutch Grand Prix, Holland's only racing driver, Carel Godin de Beaufort, was allowed to start with his central-seater RSK Spyder amid the field of "big boys" (left edge of picture). His best practice lap was 1 min 44.5 secs, against Moss's 1 min 36.2 secs. De Beaufort had asked Moss to take his Spyder round the circuit, and on his third lap Moss got down to 1 min 45.1 secs. De Beaufort thought that more familiarity with the car would have reduced the time by another 2 seconds. In this light, de Beaufort's achievement is quite remarkable, for his engine gave away 1,000 cc.

"LET'S INSTALL the higher lift camshafts then"—that was Ferry Porsche's decision for Le Mans. But the weather was unkind and the rains kept away, leaving only a hot and thundery summer sky. Of 53 starters 13 made the winning post, with not a single Porsche among them. Never had defeat been so complete as on this occasion.

AFTER 13 HOURS and 13 minutes the troubles ran riot: the Maglioli/
Herrmann car had already dropped out at 9 pm, and all the other works cars
were in trouble within the forecast 14 hours. All suffered crankshaft breakage
and after 13 hours and 45 minutes von Trips' car rolled into the pits, the last
one to retire (bottom right). At the top we see him taking over from Bonnier
shortly after midnight, when no-one guessed how depressingly the day would
end. Porsche's last hope, the two private Spyders of Kerguen/Lacaze and Hugus/
Erikson also blew up.

FERRY PORSCHE
always tremendously
terested in the happen
at Le Mans and was alv
ready with help and ad
(see page 75). Only in
early hours of Sur
morning did he snatc
little sleep in the noisy
but his wife next to him
no rest.

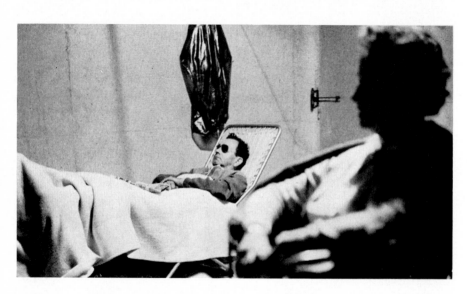

E GRAND PRIX OF BERLIN on August 1 1959 was
Behra's fateful day. Whilst the south curve was dry, a
dery rain beat down on the brick-paved steepness of the
h curve and made it into a skating rink. Everyone waited
ain for the postponement of the start. Anton von Döry's
der had already spun on the second lap in the north curve,
on the third de Beaufort disappeared over the banking while
crowd yelled in dismay. Amazingly, de Beaufort not only
ived, but—and no-one expected this—he even continued
ng. The next lap spelled the end for Behra, whose car
oshed backwards along the lip of the banking until it was
ped forever by a concrete post. Behra died of a cracked
l—below we see him on his last lap behind Count von
ps.

THE RACE continued. Von Trips (23) and Jo Bonnier (22) are overtaking Buxton in the Lotus (26) and they must all have been wondering at this spot—which we have known for a long time as a wrongly-built banking—about Behra's fate, whose wrecked car they are just passing (left).

Porsche withdrew their cars from Sundays' single-seater race after Behra's death. Our picture (below) shows him in his own car during practice next to Count von Trips in a works machine on the very spot that was to seal his fate. The big wheels give a clue to the enormous centrifugal forces which the chassis had to cope with.

1960

AIRFIELD RACES became more and more fashionable. The Americans were responsible for this because they loaned their formerly German and only partially used airfields free of charge to the organizers. This is the one at Pferdsfeld, near Bad Kreuznach, and such events soon became popular for here one could get up to things without danger, things which were hardly to be recommended on normal circuits if one wanted to get the car home in one piece. An "excursion" into the infield, a "tête a queue" or even two did not necessarily result in bashed-up bodywork, but only influenced the stop-watch. Those who did not have the ability to remember on the flat and seemingly endless concrete stretches where the ideal line or the braking point lay would never score a win, no matter how quickly they changed gear or accelerated.

Here, many could stamp out elementary faults and get ready for proper circuits, which do not forgive the nonsenses perpetrated on an airfield. Here one learned how to "add more lightness" to the cars; large numbers of Porsches met and everyone took it all terribly seriously. Any sum asked was paid gladly for a few extra horsepower. One wanted to have a go with big racing numbers on the doors, to be photographed, to buy the pictures and stick them lovingly into special albums, together with the newspaper reports. And when the photographer mentioned to his American hosts that he wished for better vantage points than mere pedestrian ones, they brought from God knows where a multi-ton vehicle with a hydraulic arm, on the platform of which one would be lifted 35 feet above the track. They were paradise-like times, but unfortunately, like all these once-in-a-while things, they now only remain a memory.

WHAT HAPPENED on this Le Mans Sunday in the Porsche pit could well have been called a public funeral, what with the ringing of church bells and the thousands of spectators. Here (below) we see Storz (left) and Schmitt, the two most competent engine specialists, trying to dismember the burning hot RS-60 of Jo Bonnier and Graham Hill in full public view. It was a last desperate attempt to get back at least one of the four big Spyders into the race, after the other three had given up the ghost. The funny remarks during the flag parade before the start (left) came true: let's hope there won't be a funeral. It was all in vain, for the diagnosis was soon clear—a faulty head gasket due to overheating. It was a pity the towel was thrown in at that moment, because fitting a new piston would have completed the public spectacle and created a storm of approval, even for a car that was hopelessly beaten. How useful this could have been became clear during the next few hours of this gruelling race.

WHILST THE bearded Swede, Jo Bonnier, had become resigned and Graham Hill's eyes were elsewhere (right), the 30,000 francs for the victor in the Index of Performance were still within reach of the Porsche drivers Barth and Seidel, whose 1.5 litre Spyder was running second in the Index a few hours before the finish. But then came the news from Klauser, for years the time-keeping boss in the Porsche pit: "Number 39 is overdue!" As if struck by lightning all heads turned in the direction of "Maison Blanche" (see page 84) from whence 39 slowly appeared. The gearbox had overheated, the bearings had given up and only 1st gear was still usable—and then only if the driver held it in. After a brief council of war Barth was told to carry on for another three-quarters of a lap, then to stop and attempt a last lap 15 minutes before the finish, which he managed. The last hope now rested on the GTL Carrera (35) of Linge/Walter who is here (below right) about to restart at 4.50 am after changing drivers and refuelling. He saved the honour of the house and won the 1,600 class, finishing 11th in the general classification.

FOG, RAIN and cold could not stop 250,000 spectators from visiting the "Ring" for the 1,000 kilometres race. They were not disappointed, for seldom had the Eifel mountains witnessed such exciting sport. Practice brought the first sensation: Bonnier covered a lap in the 1.7 litre Porsche in 9 min 43.6 secs and seven seconds later came Stirling Moss in the "Birdcage" Maserati, in front of the big Ferraris, Astons and Maseratis.

Our two top pictures demonstrate the constantly changing weather conditions—they were both taken from the same spot. On the left von Trips in the Ferrari is being hard pressed by Jo Bonnier, with visibility good at that moment, though the surface was slippery. Minutes later there is fog again, with visibility reduced to 30–40 yards, and from the grey curtain there approaches the Carrera (84) of Braun/Schwarz, then the privately owned RS 60s of Walter/Losinger and Frère/de Beaufort, and finally the Abarth-Carrera of Koch/Straussberg.

Behind the winners Moss/Gurney came Bonnier/Gendebien—here (left) in a full drift on the "Schwalbenschwanz"—in second position. Their overall average was only 0.43 mph slower than that of the winners, and Herrmann/Trintignant slipped their Porsche into fourth place. Altogether, this event was a great Porsche success: with three class wins in the 2 and 1.6 litre sports car class and in the 1.6 litre GT category, they could be more than satisfied.

NO SOLITUDE races are complete without Ursel von Hanstein's splendidly laid-on evening parties in and outside their house, Kräherwald. Apart from those prominent in motor racing, this year's guests included the pretender to the Spanish throne, Don Juan, whom we see here (below) with the host and hostess and, bottom, facing an enormous bucketful of Swabian potato salad, Marianne and Joachim Bonnier load their plates with chicken and other goodies. It was early in the morning when the last ones left the "battlefield", and when the starter sent the field off (right) the traditionally good Solitude weather prevailed. If Jim Clark's engine had not died from overheating,

he would have won this Formula 2 event just as certainly as he did the Junior one.

This led to an exciting duel between von Trips in the only Ferrari and the Porsche "armada", driven by Hans Herrmann, Jo Bonnier, Graham Hill and Dan Gurney. Here is Bonnier in front of Hill and Herrmann in the Glemseck curve, followed by von Trips, Jim Clark, Gurney and the multiple champion of motor cycling, John Surtees, who showed in practice that soon he would also master four-wheel racing. His car was the one used by Stirling Moss in the previous spring at Aintree, and with which he won so convincingly for Porsche.

ALTHOUGH the race was not a Porsche victory, it provided some excellent sport and many exciting battles. Surtees was singularly unlucky (bottom), since he was unable to finish due to engine trouble, yet three hours previously he had won convincingly on the 4 cylinder MV Agusta (below). After Clark dropped out, having led for a long while with the Lotus, von Trips and Hans Herrmann, who knows every stone on this circuit, duelled fiercely. "It took lap after lap," he said afterwards, "before I could catch him." Gurney (22) drove this Porsche (bottom right) with the flatter nose and a box-shaped tail into fifth place and Herrmann finished in second spot.

1961

THE FIRST Formula 1 event for Porsche took place in Brussels on April 9 1961. Although this memorable occasion ended disappointingly (at the end of the three heats, each 62.2 miles long, neither of the cars driven by Bonnier and Gurney was left in the running) there were still a lot of splendid battles which provided great interest for the spectators. The race demonstrated to the Zuffenhausen works that it could also hold its own in the Formula 1 field—and that was all that they expected from the Brussels Grand Prix.

Gurney having dropped out of the first heat after very few laps, due to gearbox troubles, Bonnier briefly took the lead after the start of the second heat (top right), having had an excellent run in the first. But then fate took a hand, in the shape of Surtees in the Yeoman Credit Cooper, who had carved his way rapidly through the middle field. On the 11th lap, coming out of the village of Strombeek, he was so close to Bonnier that on braking he was unable to avoid slightly touching the Swede's car. What happened next is shown in

the pictures. Surtees had to apologize and Marianne expressed what her husband meant—let's forgive and forget. Von Hanstein made this comment: "Surtees will be the driver of the year—there is no doubt about it."

FOR PORSCHE, Brussels was by way of being an advance skirmish, and Syracuse was the dress rehearsal. It was still not a question of world championship points but of acquiring valuable experience, without which even large racing stables cannot manage. Among all the Grand Prix drivers pictured here, and led by Gurney at the start (above), was a virtually unknown young Italian in the driving seat of the lone Ferrari. He was Giancarlo Baghetti, son of a wealthy family, here (right) in fifth position and driving beautifully. He shot into the lead on the 24th lap and won his first Formula 1 race at the age of 25, a truly brilliant performance.

THE DEBUT of the eight-cylinder car in the Monaco Grand Prix did not take place as planned. Instead Porsche brought the four-cylinder cars with indirect fuel injection, new chassis and slightly changed bodies to the Principality, whose tortuous circuit was thought to be ideal for the cars. Neither Bonnier nor Gurney were able in practice to qualify for the first two rows of the grid. To compare times, Moss achieved 1 min 39.1 secs, Bonnier 1 min 40.3 secs, Gurney 1 min 40.6 secs and Herrmann 1 min 41.1 secs. On the standing lap at the station hairpin (below) one could see in fourth and fifth positions the first of the three Porsches; Herrmann was last but one. Clark led from Moss but could not beat him, for he drove brilliantly.

NOW THAT EVERYTHING was at stake the Porsche still seemed large and clumsy, in contrast to the plastic-bodied Lotus from whose graceful lines the suspensions extended like spider's legs. What the fuel injected engine gained in torque, the big frontal area absorbed and soon other troubles became apparent. Herrmann's and Bonnier's new cars had no baffles in their narrow side tanks to prevent fuel from splashing about as they gradually emptied, and this caused air bubbles to interrupt the fuel supply when the drivers had to brake. It was soon sorted out, back home, after the race. Bonnier (2), who for a time took second spot behind Moss, came to a standstill with a sound engine. Here we see him (left) about to enter the viaduct, in the hairpin at the railway station (bottom centre), and (below) accelerating out of that corner. Gurney (4) is pictured (bottom left) in the old Syracuse car at the railway corner, and above him Hans Herrmann just before the viaduct.

WHAT WAS NOT so obvious on the narrow town circuit of Monaco became very apparent indeed on the faster circuit of Zandvoort amongst the sand dunes in Holland. Already, shortly after the start, the cars driven by Gurney, Bonnier and Herrmann proved to be clearly inferior from the engine and chassis point of view. At the end of the race Gurney (7), one lap behind and in tenth place in front of Bonnier, was in agreement with the latter that on the limit they no longer had full control over their cars. A fascinating duel for the duration of the race was fought between de Beaufort with his old carburettor engine and Herrmann with the works fuel-injection car (below) which de Beaufort won. Together with his rival he provided the spice for those not satisfied with the Richie Ginther (Ferrari) versus Stirling Moss (Lotus) duel.

"TOMORROW'S HEAT will be the decider," said Raymond Roche on the evening preceding this memorable race—the French Grand Prix at Rheims—and how right he was proved to be. When he flagged off the 25 cars for their 52 laps the thermometer showed almost 55 degrees centigrade in the sun. Ginther (18) took the lead from von Trips (20) and Phil Hill (16), Moss (26), Graham Hill (22), Surtees (40), Innes Ireland (6) and Clark (8). The two Porsches, led by Gurney, were in the middle of the field. But after two thirds of the race was run all the forecasts were wrong. Three of the highly favoured Ferraris were no longer in the leading positions, but during the last 12 laps there was the sort of bitter battle that made it worth bearing the heat. The

sweaty faces of the principal actors could only be seen momentarily at the Thillois hairpin and a tri-partite contest had begun. Bonnier (10), Gurney (12) and Baghetti (50) managed to bring even the very last of the heat-exposed spectators under their spell. The likelihood of the 1960 four-cylinder cars actually winning a Grand Prix—something no-one dared even mention—came very near to being a possibility but in the last thousand yards something happened which the experts would never have believed credible. Baghetti, still something of a greenhorn in this field of aces and who arrived first at the Thillois curve, decelerated at its exit, moved over slightly, and immediately Gurney, who had been slipstreaming him, fell into Baghetti's trap by moving out of his slipstream. This mistake, which the experienced Gurney should never have made, cost him victory a few seconds later. But let us not anticipate: instantly in his graceful car, the Italian "attached" himself to the fat Porsche at a yard's distance, saved 500 rpm and remained thus until some 200 yards before the finish. Only then did he leave his "tow", Gurney, pass him, and win easily by a car's length. Despite this, Gurney managed to finish in front of Clark, Ireland and Bruce McLaren.

THIS YEAR the Solitude race again fulfilled every expectation, except that Porsche were still unable to hoist the flag of victory. Although they fielded their best people, with Bonnier and Gurney, they could not manage to beat the Scottish driver Innes Ireland with his Lotus. Five of the cars were never more than 20 or 40 yards apart during the entire 25 laps. The lower series of pictures shows this exciting situation during the 23rd, 24th and 25th laps. No 1 is Ireland, with Bonnier (9) and Gurney behind, and under the finishing banner it was Ireland by a nose. All this crowned an eagerly awaited yearly event, to the success of which Porsche always contributed. This time it was a swabian supper at the Glemstal Hotel by the circuit, to which Porsche issued invitations. Here (top left) Bonnier delivers the drivers on a diesel tractor and (centre left) Moss flirts with Mrs von Hanstein, whilst talking shop with H. U. Wieselmann, editor of the motoring publication, "Auto, Motor and Sport".

THE GRAND PRIX OF EUROPE at the Nürburgring was unlucky for Porsche, though the front row grid position which Bonnier had achieved in practice gave many Porsche enthusiasts good reason to be hopeful. Their hope turned to disappointment, however, for Bonnier ran out of road, suffered tyre trouble and lost a lot of time having a new wheel fitted. This put him back into 17th position and the following chase to regain a good place did his engine no good at all. Herrmann also fell back hopelessly with clutch trouble. Porsche's last trump, Gurney (below) touched Graham Hill's BRM, and a bent rear wheel mounting resulted in a slowed-up Porsche. He finished in seventh position and crossed the line more than 3 minutes after the winner—Moss. Richie Ginther with his Ferrari (5) is shown still leading Gurney (top right) and finished 8th, while the competent Mairesse (leading) was unplaced in his Ferrari. Bottom right: Some mechanics will go to extremes to get things right!

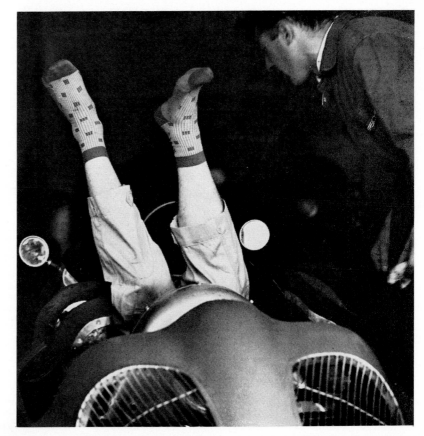

45ᴬ TARGA FLORIO

30 APRILE 1961

"MACCHINA IN ARRIVA!" Who does not know this shout and the accompanying bang from the cannon which make thousands look up from the artichoke fields of Madonie, for it announces the arrival of yet another car at the Targa Florio pits after completing the 72 kilometre (44.4 mile) lap. In this explosive atmosphere everyone awaited the winner of the 45th Targa, Stirling Moss in Porsche no 136. Radio and television reporters, their voices tremulous with emotion, yelled his name into their microphones, but the seconds ticked on and Moss did not arrive. His 65 seconds lead over the pursuing von Trips in a new 2.4 litre Ferrari crumbled further and further. When his lead had totally evaporated and guesswork became a certainty, news came that Moss had stopped exactly three kilometres (1.86 miles) from the finish with a seized back axle. The car was immovable and could not even be pushed. Frenetic Italian rejoicing accompanied Count Trips' win.

MOSS, HILL and Bonnier are pictured with their cars (bottom left). Hardly anywhere in the world is the backdrop for a driver change more colourful or exciting. Is it the air, the landscape or the colours of this island? We don't know the answer, but make our annual pilgrimage to this, the last true road race of the 20th century. The picture above shows Gurney taking over from Bonnier in the Porsche that took second place.

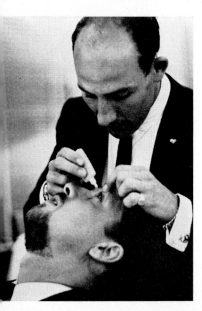

IT MIGHT WELL BE a biblical scene but for our cabriolet in the picture (bottom previous page). This is a Sicilian family who, with kith and kin, take to the mountains for the summer and include even live chickens suspended by the legs. A few yards alongside there is fresh red paint on the boundary stones of the road which help the drivers to pick out the more hairy corners, of which there is no shortage on the 44.4 mile lap! Let us say a word of praise and appreciation for the private entrants, who year after year make their way to the Madonie circuit at considerable expense. In particular Swabian Paul-Ernst Straehle, here busy cleaning the windscreen (far left), prior to handing over to his co-driver von Hanstein. Top left is Moss waving to us on a corner where all the other drivers are in urgent need of both hands on the wheel, while (above) his co-driver Graham Hill is at the wheel. Pictured left is the sporting Moss putting eyedrops into his team mate Jo Bonnier's eyes, during an evening party at the fashionable Mondello resort, where the winner is feted.

PORSCHE CAME to the 1,000 Kilometres at the Nürburgring with still more horsepower than the previous year, and with no less a driver than Stirling Moss. He was expected to overcome obvious weaknesses in the car, but this did not materialize. Wieselmann of "Auto, Motor and Sport," wrote: "They hoped to bridge the time until the full development of the eight cylinder with the trusty four cylinder which had served faithfully for so many years. But after Monaco, Zandvoort and today's race it does not look as if their hopes will be realized. Despite cool and damp weather two of the three works cars retired with blown-up engines over the short distance of 1,000 Kilometres." The third was in poor condition and managed 10th place. Here we have (top left) Hahnl/Zick (71) and Koch/Leinweber (74) in their Abarth-Carreras leading the experimental Carrera of Linge/Greger in the south loop, with Moss shown below (20). Rodriguez (5) has just passed the Walter/Müller Spyder (above), before entering the right-hander at "Brünnchen". Moss is still running and so is Gurney's machine but the faces of the co-drivers Hill and Bonnier (left) show that things are not right. Bottom left is Marianne Bonnier.

THIS YEAR'S MOTTO for Le Mans was "to finish" and by way of
weapons Ferry Porsche had decreed that tame, shell-bearing engines, that is
to say Carreras, were to be used. Understandably after two years of defeat,
the normal Le Mans spirit seemed to be lacking but, as sunshine follows rain,
from the five cars that started three finished the race, proving that the decision
to use de-tuned engines was the right one. Our top three pictures taken at
Arnage show clearly the three types that were fielded. No 33 is the open
version, driven by the Americans Holbert and Gregory, Bob Holbert (above,
left) in typically American get-up and Gregory (above, right) looking like
a schoolboy caught in a prank. They were fifth in the general classification.
No 32 was the coupé (much praised by all drivers and comfortable for the
24 hours) crewed by Barth/Herrmann, which was seventh in the general
classification. No 36 is the proven Abarth-Carrera with which Linge and
Pon managed tenth place. Left is pictured the garage at Teloché and next
to it the new race indicator tower by BP.

1962

A NEW YEAR, and the new Super 75 (foreground) stood revealed. It had a wider bonnet, more luggage room, outside fuel filler, fresh air ventilation, bigger wind-screen, more powerful windscreen wipers, electric sliding roof, larger rear screen and a double engine grille. In 1959 Porsche production amounted to 27 cars a day, in 1960 32, and now production had risen to 40. The Super 75 had a flat four engine of 1,582 cc capacity, an 8.5:1 compression ratio and gave 75 bhp at 5,000 rpm. Peak torque was 86 lbs ft at 3,700 rpm, while piston speed at 5,000 rpm was about 40 ft per sec and at 62 mph in fourth gear (3,100 rpm) about 25 ft per sec. The engine had a four-bearing crank-shaft, a central camshaft operating the valves through pushrods and rockers, air cooling by means of a fan blower, pressurised lubrication (about 10 pints capacity), a by-pass oil filter and an oil cooler. Two twin downdraught Zenith 32 NDIX carburettors were fitted, together with a mechanical fuel pump, a 10½ gallon fuel tank in the front and a 6 volt 84 amp/hour battery.

THERE WAS no need for sunbu[r]n cream or similar products when t[he] participants in the 1962 Internatio[nal] Porsche rally met in April at Zürs, on t[he] Arlberg in Austria, for they beca[me] snowbound for a few days. Some [of] them saw, probably for the first time [in] their lives, how expensive rockets a[re] fired into likely avalanches, to get t[he] snow correctly aimed downhill. What [in] the evening could be recognised [as] "Porsches under snow" became n[ext] morning a deeply buried, indefina[ble] something. The only people unimpress[ed] by all this were the ski instructors [of] Zürs. Their "Porsche 62" outlined [in] flaming torches (below) illuminated t[he] night, whilst the telephones ran red h[ot] as marooned participants telephoned [to] announce their delayed departures. A[ll] that could be staged was a slal[om] between yard-high walls of snow, a[nd] the hillclimb had to be cancelled becau[se] of the danger from avalanches. Desp[ite] all this it was a successful event and, [as] always, a pleasant change welcomed [by] everyone.

REAT INTEREST was aroused by the debut of
e eight cylinder car at Zandvoort, but admiration
ntred on the latest monocoque Lotus designed by
olin Chapman, and with it this inventive English-
an fielded the smallest Formula I racing car. After
xperimenting for two years, Porsche had at last
hieved a flat and shapely vehicle, which im-
ediately impressed with its robustness. Its frontal
ea was much smaller compared to its predecessor

and in brief it was a lucky throw, even if its first
attempt did not succeed. The fastest, with Gurney at
the wheel, only managed the third row of the starting
grid, not exactly an impressive performance. After
the start a group of three soon formed—Clark,
Graham Hill and Gurney. To begin with they
outdistanced the field and, for a few laps, all was
well for Gurney, seen below (in helmet) with Jo
Bonnier.

HAPPENED on the tenth of the 80
s: Gurney slid, put the car on the
ass, re-started and went into the pits
the next lap. He had trouble with
ar selection and it took some minutes
repair. On the 22nd lap the leaders
pped Bonnier's eight cylinder car and
final result was something very un-
pected: de Beaufort in the ancient
r cylinder car with which he had
anaged a lap at 1 min 37.4 secs in
actice, finished in sixth place, four
s behind and in front of Bonnier,
o was five laps behind the winner.

P. E. STRAEHLE gave a spectacular demonstration in the 46th Targa Florio with his privately entered Carrera. Trying hard to catch up, he touched another car at the very moment when he was fishing a slice of orange out of his "food box", thus changing gear a fraction of a second too late. His co-driver F. Hahnl was shown the black flag (above) and the stewards remained unshakeable—"out!"

THE COMPETITION DEBUT of the eight cylinder in 2 litre form could have resulted in an overall victory, and it was not the engine but the newly developed disc brakes that let the Porsches down. The open car (100) was meant for Bonnier/Gurney, but the American touched a wall on the second lap due to insufficient braking and this did not improve the car's rear suspension. The second eight cylinder, with a body like the 1961 Le Mans coupé, was entered for Vaccarella by "SSS Venezia" (108) and later Bonnier was allocated to it as co-driver. However, Ferrari won overall and also took the 2 litre sports car category. Only Linge/Herrmann in the Carrera won for Porsche, in the up to 2500 cc GT class. Posters such as these (right) in which mothers are requested to look after the children, keep doors closed, and watch the animals, exist only in Sicily, while boiled squid is available just along the circuit (bottom right).

PORSCHE'S FIRST victory in a world championship Grand Prix happened at Rouen. It was Dan Gurney, that pleasant American, father of four children, who won this high-summer battle.

No-one had dared to hope for this, because Gurney had been suffering from a feverish influenza for some days. He was not at all well and those in the know did not think he would be able to stand the strain. The acclaim and pleasure were all the greater, therefore, for him, because he knew that for the first time his parents were watching him race and, for Porsche, because he inscribed their name on the winner's roll for the first time at Rouen. Gurney, whose parents and also occasionally his wife accompanied him to the circuits that year, gave of his best. His father, for 10 years bass-baritone at the Metro-politan Opera in New York, knew from personal experience what it means to win abroad, a foreigner in a foreign car.

When the starter's flag fell on that boiling hot day for the 17 cars in the 48th Grand Prix of the Automobile Club de France, there was no let-up for man or machine. The superb forests of Elbeuf provided very little cooling and it was to be expected that incidents would occur. Gurney's practice time of 2 min 16.5 secs only qualified him for sixth place on the grid, and he reached the slowest corner of the hilly circuit, the "Virage du Nouveau Monde," in seventh place. No 8 Graham Hill, in the BRM (see next page) was in the lead, but the first engines soon went on strike and there were more pit stops than in any Grand Prix of those years.

AFTER 20 of the 54 laps the leaders were Hill, Clark, Gurney and Bonnier—Jack Brabham and Bruce McLaren having retired. Then Surtees' Ferrari dropped out and slowly things happened, as described then by Günther Molter: "Like the famous ten little nigger boys, one Britisher after the other dropped out and Gurney moved up place by place. Now he was in second position and 10 cars were still in the race."

Bonnier with the second eight cylinder car stopped at the pits to refuel (centre bottom), which caused great amazement for normally a tankful lasts for the entire Grand Prix distance. Later Bonnier retired with a faulty fuel line.

When finally the leading BRM driven by Hill stopped on the circuit, Porsche's first Grand Prix was within reach. Gurney could now slow down a little and, amid tremendous rejoicing by the Porsche mechanics, crossed the finishing line the winner. Gurney averaged 163.9 kph (101.83 mph) for a distance of 352 kilometres (218.73 miles) and Graham Hill's fastest lap was 172 kph (106.8 mph). It was thus clear that the Porsche's power output was not yet sufficient to compete with the British vehicles. At the bottom left we see the two cars in the small workshops in the centre of Rouen.

THE INCIDENT at Monaco that
the experts had always feared
happened three seconds after the
start, at the gasometer hairpin.
Mairesse, driving his Ferrari with
too much enthusiasm, caused a mass
shunt to which five cars partly or
entirely fell victim. Among them
was the sole eight cylinder Porsche
driven by Gurney (right), who was
run into from behind by Trevor
Taylor's Lotus, cracking the chassis
and displacing the engine by four
inches. The incident is the only
explanation for the miserable first
lap picture showing Bonnier
followed by Bruce McLaren, the
ultimate winner (above).

TO SHOW new owners how it is "done" Porsche used aces like Bonnier, Herrmann and Barth to familiarize customers with the secrets of their products. The Solitude circuit on Porsche's doorstep was ideal for this and the American customers who had flown to Germany to collect their cars were quite absorbed by it all.

THE TOUGHEST steeplechase in the world, the Grand National, is held at Aintree, on the outskirts of Liverpool, but Porsche's appearance there for the British Grand Prix was less successful than their previous race in France. Our pictures on pages 134 and 135 of the last minute before the start show Gurney and Bonnier on the third row of the grid and de Beaufort's four cylinder car on the third-but-last row. Twenty seconds before the start, Innes Ireland (in the front row in the right) gave a sign that he was in trouble, and Phil Hill on the lone Ferrari signalled this to the drivers behind him, so that the pack roared off and left Ireland untroubled. Gurney (left), up close behind Clark, managed to position himself well for the first fast right-hander, whilst Bonnier is still in the middle of the field.

It was a dull race and Colin Chapman made his Rouen prophecy, "We'll talk again in Aintree!" come very true. Clark, who had an unchallenged win in his Lotus, managed even to lap Gurney, for which his below-par engine was responsible. When McLaren in the Cooper slipstreamed Gurney, our camera recorded this as a seemingly eight-wheeled Porsche (right) coming towards it. The New Zealand driver passed on the 11th lap, while Bonnier never really got into the picture. De Beaufort's four cylinder car finished in 14th place, six laps behind, while Gurney, two laps behind, was 9th.

Contrary to other countries, where access to the pits is very restricted, here there was a tremendous press of people, which made it difficult for the mechanics to set the eight cylinder Porsche on British soil for the first time (below).

AINTREE

■■■ =MOTOR RACE CIRCUIT

≡≡≡ =STEEPLECHASE COURSE

CLOUDS OVER the Eifel mountains—no rarity in this region of Western Germany—characterised the 1962 German Grand Prix at the Nürburgring. The Formula 1 race was preceded by a GT event in which all classes were exceptionally well supported. As a pleasant change, the start of this supporting race was not by classes (700 to 3,000 cc) but by practice times and the wet track soon sorted the wheat from the chaff. The big GT cars were particularly interesting and, despite the awful weather, the 250,000 spectators (some of them pictured bottom right) stayed the course. In the big GT class there was, apart from a number of Ferraris, an Aston Martin to be driven by Peter Lindner, and an E Type Jaguar with Sir John Whitmore at the wheel. The 1600 class united Germany's best drivers, like H. Linge, G. Koch and F. Hahnl, but they had some quite stiff competition from the Dutchman Ben Pon. Our picture below shows him in the fast left-hander before the finishing straight, followed by Whitmore. It was also Pon who managed the fastest lap in his class at 11 min 27 secs, a speed of 119.5 kph (74.25 mph), although Herbert Linge led him across the finishing line. The almost-twice-as-powerful GTO Ferrari, handled by the Swiss K. von Csazy, recorded a fastest lap of 11 min 18.3 secs. The grid (right) shows that the fastest Porsches were Abarth-bodied, and these are, of course, much lighter than the series Carreras.

Adenau
Wehrseifen
Ex-Mühle
Bergwerk
Kesselchen
Hohe Acht
Wippermann
Kallenhard
Metzgesfeld
Karussell
Eschbach
Brünnchen
Pflanzgarten
Adenauer-Forst
Fuchsröhre
Schwalben-
schwanz
Aremberg
Schwedenkreuz
Kottenborn
Döttinger
Höhe
Nürburg
Meuspath
Flugplatz
Antoniusbuche
Quiddelbacher-
Höhe
Tiergarten
Hoch-
eichen
Start and Finish
Hatzenbach
Südschleife

THIRTY YARDS after the start of the German Grand Prix the 26 Formula 1 cars disappeared in a wall of water. The Californian Dan Gurney gave a fine display of a lightning start on the wet circuit and was still leading on the back straight (left) and further on into the "Hatzenbach" curve. Immediately behind him, and in third place, is John Surtees with the Lola, then alongside him is Graham Hill (11), who passed Gurney at the start of the third lap (below) and kept his lead to the end.

On the next page we see a group of three cars about to enter the left-hander at "Hatzenbach". Heading them are Baghetti's and Phil Hill's Ferraris in front of the second eight cylinder Porsche driven by Bonnier.

HERE WE HAVE a splendid "flying" display (facing page) by Gurney (top) and Graham Hill on one of the famous (or infamous) jumps of the "Ring", a few hundred yards before the "Karussell". Those who "take off" here must be going very fast and this is only possible if the ideal line is kept to within inches. Obviously these jumps do not come as a surprise to the top drivers, for if they did not release the throttle whilst "flying" the revs would soar to dangerous heights and the engines would succumb after three or four laps. The drivers themselves also bounce up out of their seats, as can be seen by the roll-over bars, which are normally level with the driver's crash helmets. The completely unladen rear wheels are also noteworthy, as they give an idea of the force at play after the cars land again at these extreme speeds.

1963

"WITH KLIPPAN in the air"* was this year's motto for the 1,000 kilometres on the Ring. These pictures are by way of a substitute for those who have not had the opportunity to get an aerial view and they convey, as no other viewpoint can, why this circuit is known as one of the most beautiful and difficult in the world. The outside picture on the left is of the winding lead-in to the "Schwalbenschwanz", while the middle picture shows the "Kleine Karussell" with Barth and Bonnier just coming through. From here until our third picture of the flat-out straight up to the start/finish line (top left, but outside the picture) the road is fast and leads briefly but windingly through the woods. Alongside is the main spectators' access road, with cars still on their way to the circuit.

* Klippan are safety belt manufacturers.

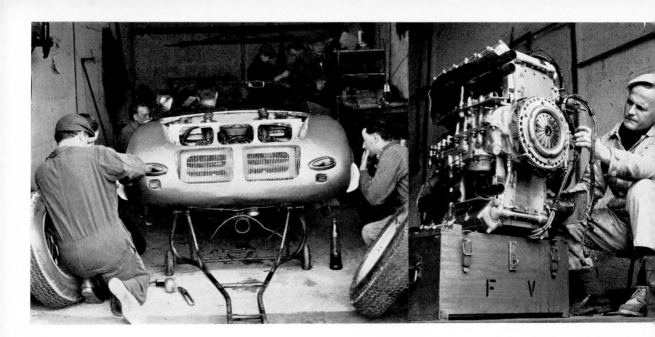

BEFORE THE START our helicopter hovered just above the pits to watch the drivers slowly taking up their positions for the Le Mans-type start. The sun was out—by no means an everyday occurrence for this spring-time race in the Eifel. Porsche had come here with a lot of confidence, after the Swedish-Italian combination Bonnier/Abate had won the 45th Targa Florio in the 2 litre prototype a few weeks before. A minute later we could hardly believe our eyes—160 yards above—when the field entered the South loop, led by the E Type Jaguar driven by Peter Lindner (top picture next page). We thought that this could not last long and so we flew along with the leader. When he passed the finish-line, still leading the 3 litre GTO Ferraris, our pilot looked at his stopwatch and yelled in my ear: "Unbelievable, he got round in 10 min 4 secs!" Lindner continued to lap at under 10 minutes in front of the Ferraris until later the car retired with engine trouble, driven by its co-driver Peter Nöcker; to the *cognoscenti* this was a sensational achievement.

No major race was complete without Porsche's top engine man Eberhard Storz, here (centre top) finishing off the Bonnier/Hill eight cylinder. Little did he know then that, after leading the race when both Parkes and Mairesse had spun their Ferraris, the sensible Hill would run the car into a ditch due to a missed gear change. This was the very ditch which had caused the downfall of many important drivers, the right-hander near "Aremberg". Storz's able hands work no longer—the 41-year-old expert was later killed while testing a car. But Hill's car (100) was not the only one in trouble because the open eight cylinder (top left) in the hands of Barth/Linge stopped on the circuit a few laps after the start with a broken drive shaft. Porsche's last hope was now centred on the works GT, a Carrera with Le Mans body (31), in the hands of Walter and Ben Pon, and also driven towards the end by the "unemployed" Linge and Barth. It finished fourth in the general classification and easily won its class.

WITH no 26, the private owners Koch and Straehle won an impressive victory in the 1,600 cc class. Here we see them (left) in the "Ex-Mühle", whilst the saviour of Porsche's honour, no 31 (above), is just about to pass a fellow competitor at the "Wippermann". Below we see the famous "Karussell", during the first lap. Peter Lindner has already passed the Döttinger Höhe, whilst the two Ferraris behind him are just moving out of the innermost curve of the corner.

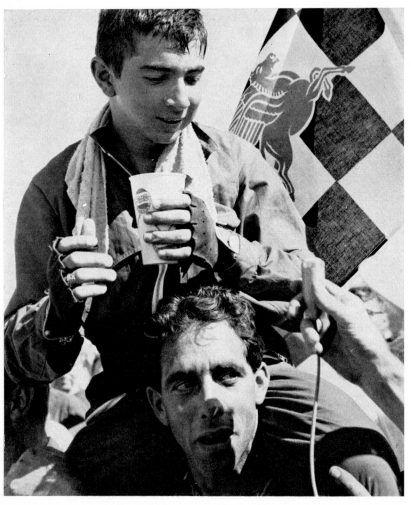

THE Porsche "bug" cannot be stopped by frontiers nor, indeed, by Continents. The famous conductor Herbert von Karajan is shown here (top left) in one of the first Spyders built for private purchase. Prince Bertil of the Swedish royal family also visited the Stuttgart works (above). The Porsche bug also infected the child prodigy Ricardo Rodriguez (far left) and the king of modellers, Michele Conti, from Milan, here (left) seen constructing exact-scale miniature Porsches. The Stuttgart graphic artist Erich Strenger (below) has made use of all this, and Porsche is indebted to him for many good catalogues, brochures and sales posters.

IN THE MAJOR international rallies privately-entered Porsches frequently scored impressive victories. One of the main events is the annual winter rally, finishing in Monte Carlo, the parc fermé of which, along the coast road, is shown above; normally this is where the Grand Prix cars roar along the quayside. Right is one of the most experienced Monte Carlo rallyists, Hans Joachim Walter, with his co-driver Ewald Stock at the control at Chambéry. Walter was fastest of all in his 2 litre Carrera in the eliminating race round the town circuit, and the car (far right) bears the imprint of this tough winter rally through the Maritime Alps. That year the Scandinavians triumphed again because of their clever snow and ice tyres. The picture (top centre) shows the Finnish Kelhu tyres with built-in studs, and below them the normal Finnish spikes.

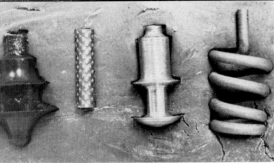

PAT MOSS (above), this year for the first time Mrs Carlsson and normally having practically a "season ticket" for the "Coupe des Dames", was unlucky. She was eliminated through engine trouble and is here seen "crowning" H. J. Walter during the presentation ceremony which took place in Monte Carlo. Huschke von Hanstein is between them.

THE MARATHON of the Road is what they called the rally that hid behi
three words: "Liège-Sofia-Liège". Anyone involved in motoring sport loo
upon victory in this long-distance event as his crowning ambition. Nevertheld
competitors have foundered prematurely on the sheer physical requirements
this event. Only those who have driven five days and four nights with only
hour's enforced stop in Sofia, against tough opposition, dust, heat, fatigue and
clock, really know what these three words mean! Those who arrived in Liè
within the time limit had reason to be proud. The winner is fêted like a king, a

erwards the hardship is forgotten while only the memory of an adventure that nges every year and recalls the dawn of motoring remains. Here there is no h thing as a malicious smile if another competitor slides into a ditch. Here re is always a helping hand, even at the risk of being delayed, for the same amity might well befall you on the next corner. Only those who have stood ne before God and the world on a mountain road in Macedonia or Montenegro, th the car in the ditch, and have waited, shivering, for the dawn and the passing le cart of a local peasant, know what help means at a time like this!

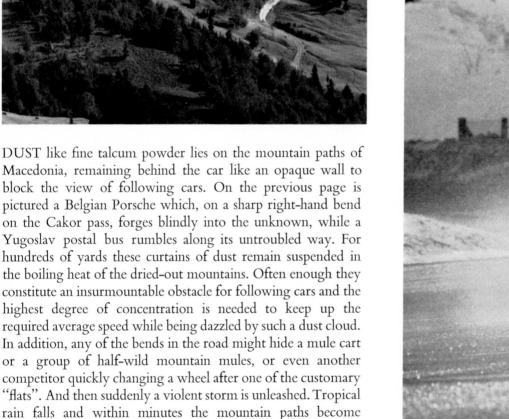

DUST like fine talcum powder lies on the mountain paths of Macedonia, remaining behind the car like an opaque wall to block the view of following cars. On the previous page is pictured a Belgian Porsche which, on a sharp right-hand bend on the Cakor pass, forges blindly into the unknown, while a Yugoslav postal bus rumbles along its untroubled way. For hundreds of yards these curtains of dust remain suspended in the boiling heat of the dried-out mountains. Often enough they constitute an insurmountable obstacle for following cars and the highest degree of concentration is needed to keep up the required average speed while being dazzled by such a dust cloud. In addition, any of the bends in the road might hide a mule cart or a group of half-wild mountain mules, or even another competitor quickly changing a wheel after one of the customary "flats". And then suddenly a violent storm is unleashed. Tropical rain falls and within minutes the mountain paths become torrents. Those whose cars are not watertight beware! Sitting in water, dressed only in swimming trunks and without a dry

stitch in the car, one presses on to the next human habitation. No-one could guess then that the Liège-Sofia-Liège was going to be run for the last time the following year, for in 1964 they buried this, the last, biggest and toughest European rally. The Yugoslav government saw in it a danger to its tourist traffic, after at first putting their entire road system at the organizer's disposal. On the German side, it was the Bavarian police who checked competitor's speeds by radar, found them too high and forbade the use of Bavarian roads. Our last picture on this page shows a French competitor on the Solitude circuit during the Solitude-Charbonnières rally.

1964

THE WORLD debut of the 2 litre GTS type 904 in the 12 hour race at Sebring resulted in only 20th place for Barth/Linge due to clutch trouble, and this was a defeat of some importance because of Porsche's very considerable exports to the United States. Therefore, everything was done at Zuffenhausen to ensure that no repetition occurred in the 48th Targa Florio, all the more so because the 904 promised to sell well on the European market, too. For the first time Ford decided to take part in the Sicilian adventure, which was even further reason to prepare with the utmost care. Porsche's overall victory and second, sixth and seventh places would have been even more note-worthy if the Ferrari works team, the salt in this particular soup, had not been absent. For the first time in the rich history of this traditional Sicilian event, a local man, Baron Pucci, was the winner.

SIX OF THE 72 kilometres (44.7 miles) of this fascinating mountain circuit have been covered when the cars, on full chat, whoosh through the village straight of Cerda (see page 157). Wide and comfortable lie the green and prickly artichoke fields (above) as the cars thunder past the last houses of the village to disappear seconds later around the bend. Top left we see Linge taking over from Balzarina. In the final result they were only 13 minutes slower than the winning car. Vianini (bottom left) was unlucky, having crashed on the first lap, and without this "emergency bandage" would not even have reached the pits. Pictured left is Graham Hill drifting his car round one of the corners.

THE EUROPEAN DEBUT of the 904 was an outstanding success, only mitigated by the fact that the two favourites, the eight-cylinder cars driven by Bonnier/Hill and Maglioli/Barth, dropped out, or were not fully competitive. Bonnier suffered irreparable drive shaft problems after putting up fastest practice lap with a time of 41 min 14 secs; at that time the second car, with Barth driving (top right) was leading and three of the first five cars were Porsches. When Maglioli took over fate decreed that it would take 20 minutes to put right rear suspension troubles, and this put the 904 driven by Bulgari/Grana in the lead. But this car also dropped out on the sixth lap and the happy winners were Colin Davis—son of the famous driver/journalist Sammy Davis—and Baron Pucci (a Sicilian, born and living in Palermo and something of a local celebrity). Bottom right is Pucci with his arm raised, while the nephew of the Targa Florio's founder, Vincenzo Florio, is half hidden behind. The picture below shows Pucci in the winning car, one kilometre before the finishing line.

FIVE OF THE 12 Ferraris that started retired, but five out of five Porsche GTS Carreras crossed the finishing line after 24 hours at Le Mans as fit as fiddles and ready—so the experts said—for another 24 hours. This is an important point, for no other motor sporting contest influences sales figures for such a long time and this alone is the reason why the works spares no expense or effort to bring really superbly prepared vehicles to the starting line.

As at the Nürburgring, Fords made their debut here and won the GT class first time out with a Cobra. Looked at from this point of view, Ferrari's absence from that year's Targa Florio was more than understandable.

Porsche today sells over 50 per cent of their production in the USA; good workmanship and durability are not the least of their qualities. The fact that the two works cars of Barth/Linge and Davis/Mitter dropped out with clutch trouble barely made any odds. Until then, they had led the important Index of Performance.

IS IT THE disparity between power output and the ability of the materials to withstand the strain that manifests itself here? For on the Mulsanne Straight the 2 litre prototypes were almost as fast as the 3.3 litre Ferraris. If this is so it gives rise to the thought that on the "Ring" the 1,000 Kilometres take far less than 10 hours, and the same applies to the Targa—yet this period in time was reached here at Le Mans at 2 am when Barth dropped out. That the reasoning seems right was proved by the fact that Porsches entered the GTS types, where such a desirable relationship between power output and lasting ability is manifest. No driver, no matter how able, can compensate for any lack of this relationship if he wants to last out the 24 hours. The night was bitterly cold and the time-keepers and pit personnel sat swathed in blankets on the windy pit counters, staring in the direction of Maison Blanche and at the frown of Huschke von Hanstein, who had then no idea how brilliantly his cars would finish (see previous page).

THIS YEAR'S 1,000 Kilometres at the "Ring" were not run under a lucky star, although Porsche's chances, based on good practice times, seemed good enough. But troubles and tragedy prevailed: at over 124 mph a private owner, R. W. Moser (top left) lost control and crashed fatally. Barth was very lucky when, running-in new brake pads, he lost the lot on braking at the South curve, the car somersaulting over and becoming a total write-off. Ruby and Pillette also ran out of road in their 904 GTS and during the race Colin Davis, winner of the Targa Florio, slid into the ditch at Aremberg. Clearly, the 904 was too fast for its owners as far as a number of drivers were concerned, for it could put up lap times comparable to those of Fangio in 1955 with a 3 litre eight cylinder car. It is a sensational car, seemingly glued to the road surface, but also quite unforgiving when tried beyond the limit.

MARANELLO had brought its most powerful battle-force and, for the first time, a works 4.2 litre Ford tried its luck on the uphill-and-down-dale Eifel circuit. No quarter was given or, indeed, asked for. Our picture shows some of the cars on their first lap—taken from the Flugplatz—here "led" by the car that eventually won, no 144 driven by Scarfiotti and Vaccarella. However, at that moment Surtees' proto-type Ferrari had already entered the Aremberg curve.

The Ford GT with Phil Hill at the wheel is betwe the "pincers" of the prototypes of Bonnier and Bart Their cars left the road with all four wheels at t "jumps". Driving was tough, and the now faster Ri took its toll. Neither the favourite Surtees nor the fa Porsches were still racing at the finish, but the priva owners Pon/Koch, with their 904, saved the firn bacon and were third in the general classification.

HE LIVED and died with Porsche: Carel Godin de Beaufort, Master of Maaren and Maarsbergen, and the last scion of an old Dutch aristocratic family. The bell tolled for him in the final practice period for the Grand Prix of Germany on August 2 1964, driving his old four-cylinder Formula 1 Porsche. Always cheerful and ready for any lark, strong as an ox and ever willing to help, he seemed part and parcel not only of the works in Zuffenhausen but of the circuits of the world too. Experience had taught him many lessons, and he had covered hundreds of thousands of miles in 'planes, ships and cars; no-one thought he would ever die at the wheel. Trying to prevail against the eight-cylinder cars, he overdid it in his four-cylinder Porsche. Now he lies in his moated castle, never to be forgotten within its ancient walls. He truly deserved to be amongst us still.

THIS YEAR again, the European Mountain Championship was characterized by colourless and unexciting heats. Edgar Barth, (left), who seemed to have a season ticket for the Championship, won everywhere and also here at Rossfeld. Of the two available eight-cylinder cars, he chose the Elva (far left, top) the ultra-light chassis of which had to be reinforced to cope with the powerful engine. This exceedingly low vehicle, weighing only 520 kilos (1146 lb), had fantastic acceleration and seemed positively menacing compared with the normal mountain championship car (bottom left) which had been entrusted to Herbert Müller, the little red haired Swiss driver. Here and in the following heats, Porsche noted the young Bavarian "light weight", Toni Fischhaber, who, with a Lotus-BMW, put up in practice the same time as Müller in the eight-cylinder car (3 min 16.42 secs). However, he spun during the first run and therefore could no longer influence second position. This talented Bavarian needed to learn a little more control and reliability before the way to a works drive could open up for him. As always in those days, Sepp Greger won his class in a Carrera (below).

THE CLASSIC Le Mans circuit (top, far left), the steepness of the Col de Turini (bottom, far left), the winding town circuit of Pau, (left), the many passes of the Maritime Alps (centre left), the airfield in Cognac (bottom), and the up-and-down Clermont-Ferrand track: these were only some of the stages in the 13th, and unfortunately last, "Tour de France Automobile", for which Porsche fielded a full works team for the first time. For those in the know, this was something of a sensation and seemingly the beginning of a new era. We had never doubted that these small, nimble and rapid cars would have all the qualities for rally, long-distance and circuit participation, and this confidence was fully justified in this 6,000 kilometre, (3,720 mile) event. In the handicap class, Porsche came first and second, and on scratch third, fourth, fifth and sixth. This result surprised them as much as it did those who had doubted their potential. Although their service en route was not as efficient as that of other works, whose experience went back many years, the Porsche people demonstrated their rapid adaptability. Praise is due here particularly to the mechanics, who coped with the incredible situations, and it was largely due to them that all GTSs—with one exception because of family reasons—reached the finish in Nice. Below are pictured: Klass, Buchet, Linge and Wütherich—the principal Porsche team drivers.

1965

HERE WE HAVE Böhringer and Wütherich in a snowstorm on the Col de Turini. What began with the works participation in the 1964 Tour de France and had given rise to the hope that Porsche would take up the cudgels against the Anglo-American phalanx, seemed to come true when those two drivers managed to get the relatively new 904 GTS through bad weather conditions and against tough opposition into second spot in the 34th Monte Carlo Rally. This was all the more meritorious since serious critics had viewed the attempt as hopeless. Very noteworthy also was the somewhat daring entry of the brand-new type 911 (Linge/Falk), who won their class. All this certainly was not to be under-estimated from the point of view of its influence on car sales. To try for the European Rally Championship was therefore obvious, but hopes were disappointed for, apart from the Spanish rally, no Porsche was up front in any of the championship events, not even in the Coupe des Alpes, where the Finn Toivonen was only placed 21st. However, the two types proved that they had good potential even under the toughest winter conditions.

EN BEFORE the first common control at ambéry was reached, the snowstorm in the French ra put paid to many hopes. Choosing the wrong rting place resulted in many competitors not ching Chambéry—yet this was only one of the any pitfalls. Some had rain, others had three yard sibility due to thick snow, and were unable to see e signposts. Others again, like Linge/Falk (left top and bottom) had collected many penalty points before leaving Chambéry. Böhringer/Wütherich also collected penalties—here they are (above and below) after the time control at Castellane at the end of the special stage over the Col de Leques (Wütherich stows the helmets, whilst Böhringer refuels). The cheerful Böhringer is also pictured in his less hazardous occupation of hotel keeper.

OR THE FIRST TIME in seven years there was
excitement and battle for the title of European
Mountain Champion, albeit only in respect of one
competitor, Ludovico Scarfiotti, with his Dino
Ferrari. After the resounding results of Porsche in 1958
the event had sunk into unimportance, and year after
year Zuffenhausen took the Championship back with
them without really having to try hard. But now the
financially independent Italian, who had only one
example of the V6 2 litre prototype at his disposal,
brought his weight to bear on the contest. The moment
he appeared, first at Trento-Bondone (the Mont
Ventoux and Rossfeld events had been won by Hans
Herrmann in an Abarth and Mitter with a Porsche),
he took charge of the whole scene. Unquestionably,
Mitter's eight cylinder 2 litre prototype had enough
"horses", but with its relatively old-fashioned chassis
the power could not be fully used. Whilst Ferry

Porsche was on holiday, his nephew, the 38-year-old
Ferdinand Piëch, decided to build a new vehicle using
important parts from a Lotus Formula 1 chassis in the
hope of being able, even at the last minute, to cut into
the winning performance of the Dino. At Ollon-
Villars (left) it became clear that this ad-hoc construction was by no means ripe enough to prevail against
the Dino. Scarfiotti, shown here with Piëch (wearing
hat, above) and his engineers, became mountain
champion, and Porsche lost a domain that they had
had on firm "lease" for years. Had the new car, with
its improved chassis, been ready at the beginning of
the year, then maybe Mitter could have repeated what
von Trips had earlier achieved in such a masterful
manner.

The Swiss H. Müller, with the Mont Blanc Massif
as a background, is shown on his way to a class
victory, (top left).

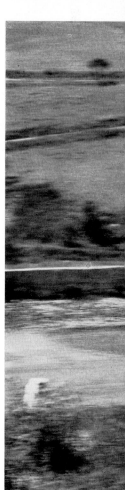

"IF SHEER ugliness wins, then there is no question that the eight cylinder prototype of Davis and Mitter must come first in the 49th Targa Florio". Thus spoke the pundits prior to the race... The car weighed only 600 kilos (1322 lb) and was propelled by 235 bhp, therefore it had a strong chance of success. Despite this, the record holder Bonnier refused to drive the car since he was not happy with its road holding. The Anglo-German pair did, however, take second place with no 182, the ugly duckling, and this against four works Ferraris and the twice-as-big Ford GT. Bonnier/ Graham Hill won with the eight cylinder and Klass/Pucci with a Carrera GTS were fifth. A very respectable result, one might say. Left top: A policeman whistles in indignation because the author is snapping him whilst carrying out his duties. Left: Campo Felice, one of the three villages on the circuit, and Maglioli's six cylinder in the winding part of Kilometre 38.

THE 23RD OF MAY, nine seconds past 9 am and 63 cars (above) are on the first of the 1,000 Kilometres of the Nürburgring. Practice times and the entry justified the high expectations—for the first time there was a powerful American Ford and Cobra contingent among the runners. One viewed the three works Ferraris with some respect, for the Porsche team was a bit lame at the start, due to the slightly modified Targa "ugly duckling" having been written off by Mitter in practice. The picture on the right (car number 21)—one of the few that there are of this now non-existent car—shows Mitter on the apex of the Wehrseifen left-hander, which is only taken correctly if there is some contact between the hedge and the bodywork. Top right is shown the eight-cylinder prototype which, with Bonnier at the wheel and co-driven by Jochen Rindt, finished third in the general classification eight minutes behind the winning Ferrari.

THE THIRD PLACE of Bonnier and Rindt was only gained because the 1.6 litre engine of the brilliantly driven Dino Ferrari (Bandini/Vaccarella) was obviously losing power towards the end of the race. This exceptionally attractive Italian car was followed home by the two six cylinder cars of Maglioli/Linge (23, above) and Nöcker/Klass in fifth and six places. Among the first 14 finishers were six Porsches—proof yet again that the Zuffenhausen cars were not lacking in staying power. The two lower pictures were taken a few months later during the GP of Germany meeting, also on the Ring. They are of the up to 2,500 cc GT class winners—Pon (1) and Schütz.

MAJOR ATTACK by the Americans: this year
at Le Mans 11 Fords, some with 7 litre engines,
faced an equally strong armada of Ferraris. One
of the 7 litre Fords, driven by Phil Hill, had put
up a scarcely credible fastest practice lap at 227
kph (131 mph). Alongside this, the seven
Porsches (including the private ones) seemed like
harmless "also-rans", but the same could not be
said of the six Alpine-Renaults whose 1,000–
1,300 cc engines seemed hand-tailored for an
Index win. But after 90 laps there was not a
single Ford left, while Ferrari had only lost one
car, and it became clear, proved here (right) by
engineer Klauser's nodding off, that the old
unwritten laws of Le Mans were still very much
in force. All the Alpines died as well, and finally
only five Ferraris survived. The "also-rans"
pressed on among the far more powerful
machinery and finished in fourth and fifth
positions, winning the Index of Performance
with the six-cylinder car. The four-cylinder
machine gained the Consumption-Index.

1966

THE ORGANIZER'S DECISIONS in the 1966 Monte Carlo Rally were more than odd. Abruptly, the slapdash work of past years was ended, back doors to dubious interpretations of the regulations closed, and reformed verdicts announced which will forever surround this event with scandal and ridicule. The bone of contention was the lighting equipment of some highly favoured British touring cars, about whom it was also whispered that they were anything but touring. Against this, the performance expected from the Gran Turismo vehicles—to which class the Porsches belonged—was almost beyond possibilities. Porsche nevertheless decided to enter Klass/Wütherich—seen (left) in a full drift on the Col de Turini, and below on the first special stage. The bottom picture shows Schlesser/Buchet.

FOR THE jubilee race, the 50th Targa Florio, Piëch—the young chief of the experimental department—put his visiting card on the table for the first time. What had been noted at the 1965 Le Mans event was now manifest beyond doubt: the four cars were exceedingly well prepared. The fact that they did not cross the line 1-2-3 was not because of the men at the works but due to the envy and ill-will of individual drivers, and to their lack of discipline and respect for their racing manager. Yet the forecasts of a sensational victory had hardly ever been better. With the enlarged 2.2 litre eight cylinder car, G. Klass had reduced Vaccarella's previous record with the 3.5 litre Ferrari to 39 min 5 secs, a 15 second improvement. The picture on the left shows Mitter on his way to the mountain village of Collesano—the car was later totally destroyed in a collision with G. Klass. 148 is the winning Filipinetti works Carrera 6 of Mairesse/Müller, and the car at the bottom is driven by the local hero Pucci, who did not know how to cope with the wet, of which there was plenty.

AVY RAIN on the day before the race and more
ing the entire preceding night decided the author
eport the race from among the mountains at Kilo-
tre 27.5. His assumption that here the men would
sorted from the boys was amply justified because
ind each corner there lurked a very different
ard. Porsche 156, driven by Capuano/Lateri and
, driven by Bourillot/Buchet, made fifth and
hth places respectively, and are shown left passing

the wreck of a Sicilian Abarth. G. Klass (224, above)
had to abandon his ideal cornering line to miss
Biscaldi's Dino, which was facing the wrong way
after colliding with a low wall. A few laps later the
same car suffered a flat tyre and Klass himself retired
on the seventh lap with a broken suspension arm.
Road painting is very much the thing here as seen by
the picture below where some locals have inscribed
the legend "long live Vaccarella".

THE UGLY DUCKLING is dead—long live the "flounder". This was the motto introducing the new Porsche to the public during the 1,000 Kilometres at Nürburgring. From the previous years' duckling the Porsche body builders had fashioned the most aerodynamic, functional and penetrating creation that ever left their hands. But it was not the 98 cm (3 foot) high Carrera 6 but the much bigger, ultra-powerful plastic bodied and automatic Chaparral which, admittedly after the favourites had dropped out, provided the "Ring" surprise, something which neither experts nor laymen would have believed possible. Should one care to play the "if" game, then if the 2.2 litre Porsche (Rindt/Vaccarella) had not retired due to technical reasons, rain would have made an overall victory possible after the retirement of Surtees.

JHN SURTEES with the 4 litre Ferrari was 22
conds faster than the previous year in practice;
indt's 2.2 Porsche improved by 24. The only
xplanation for this was a much improved circuit.
his could be seen particularly at Hatzenbach (top
ft) and in the dreaded left-hander between
rünnchen and Pflanzgarten. Car no 17 was shared
y Bob Bondurant and Paul Hawkins. The "flying"
rototype (16) in the winding part leading to the
Karussell was in the hands of Schütz/Klass, who
held the Porsche "high jump" record at this point.
Car numbers 60 and 61 in the sports category were
entered and prepared by Ben Pon, the Dutch Porsche
concessionaire. We doubt if there is another Porsche
with such an impeccable finish as the Carrera driven
by the van Lennep brothers (above). Nöcker and
Beltoise also had to lift off at this point on the
circuit (below).

LET'S SAY IT right at the start: this year's Le Mans 24 hour race gave Porsche not *one* of its greatest successes but *the* greatest one—in a racing history which has never been devoid of success. None of the works cars competing —and the mammoth Ford factory was also represented— lost as little "blood" here as Porsche. Ferraris' retirement rate amounted to 86 per cent, a painful novelty for the Commendatore's red cars, normally so used to success.

The overall Ford victory cost them 97 per cent of their battle force, an unusually high failure rate which, because of the phenomenal number of dollars expended, can only be compared to a rocket launching at Cape Kennedy. What Ford spent here made the sums expended by Daimler-Benz on racing in 1954/55, and which one already thought exaggerated, seem more than modest. But we venture to doubt whether Mercedes would export as many cars to the USA today had they not expended these millions. Maybe the stone which Henry Ford II personally laid in the sandy soil of the Sarthe circuit will mark the start of a new era. But one thing it will not be is the mark of quality over quantity.

A 29 per cent retirement rate in these 24 hours by the manufacturing "midget" Porsche showed the Ford giant that the slogan then coined at the circuit—"America beats Europe"—was by no means proven. There is no question that the 7 litre Fords covered 4,843 kilometres (3,009.44 miles) in the 24 hours, but the Porsches, with their three-times-smaller engines, only covered a mere 174 miles less than that! This clearly shows why the world enthusiastically proclaimed a Porsche triumph, whereas it only spoke factually of a Ford victory.

THERE ARE still 1,439 minutes (or 23 hours and 59 minutes) to be run, for just a minute ago Henry Ford dispatched the pack of cars on their long journey. Of the 19 "bolides" roaring towards the "Esses" (left) only five (!) are of European origin; the American attack could hardly be more massive. None of the smaller cars has yet reached the Dunlop bridge. On the previous pages we show the two versions of the Porsche Carrera 6: car no 30 was driven by Siffert/ Davis (fourth in the general classification) and two others had this longer tail which, together with the fuel injection engine, (shown above), increased the top speed by some 6–9 mph compared to the "short" cars. In the top picture on this page we see Jo Siffert (wearing helmet) at a scheduled pit stop in the early cool of Sunday morning, when another 10 hours are still to be covered and the results are as yet quite uncertain.

WHILE the race is young and hopes are high, the cars are all running and the tension of the closely packed tens of thousands of spectators is acute, then the author has a surfeit of work. One should have twice as many arms and legs, now that picture-worthy situations abound everywhere. But this circuit is eight miles long, and before one has covered even a few, hung with cameras and equipment, the first cars are already retiring and others have withdrawn from the photogenic duelling situations to in-line-astern formations which will provide a somewhat monotonous note for the many day and night racing hours to come. The endless night falls, and with it come those endless light ribbons, whose white begins at "Maison Blanche", vanishes for seconds in front of the pits, and becomes lost, like a bloodstain, into the night. The cold and tiredness pervade the limbs—but the new dawn does finally come. Back to the pictures: before they rush through the left/right curves of the "Esses", like pearls on a string, the cars arrive at over 125 mph at the braking point (bottom left). Above are shown 32 (de Klerk/Schütz—Carrera 6); 36 (Salmon/Hobbs—Dino Ferrari) and 58 (Klass/Stommelen—Carrera 6).

The Coats of Arms of
the Mountain Rivals

Ferrari

THE DUEL for the mountain championship, exciting and fascinating right from the start, was decided by Gerhard Mitter's Porsche after the fifth of the seven qualifying events. He won with his clutch foot in plaster (above), a relic from a spectacular accident in a race at Spa, and it necessitated the fitting of a special clutch operating rail to the hill-climb car. To win with this handicap deserves praise in itself, for who knows how often and how rapidly there is the need to swop gears on the very winding, steep hill-climb from Trento to Bondone, which is 17.3 kilometres (11 miles) long, and with a Porsche engine producing 240 bhp. No less a person than Ludovico Scarfiotti, his greatest rival, took the trouble wherever they met to pay Mitter his respects.

The clearly visible stabilising fins, also known as spoilers, are clearly seen (right) on Mitter's car. They provide more road adhesion for the front wheels on this eight cylinder car, which had a shorter-than-normal wheelbase.

THE COMPANY BOSS (here, bottom left, talking to his eldest son, who is the chief stylist), and his sister Louise Piëch, could really retire. The reason is that the Porsche sons (three of whom work in the company) and four Piëch heirs, (also including three sons, one of them married to the daughter of the late Managing Director of VW, Heinrich Nordhoff), ensure that for generations to come this company will remain a healthy family business. Their own ability, plus that of their ingenious colleagues, will guarantee that this small outfit survives in an era of large industrial concerns. Two of the youngest "children" are the Type 911S (left) and the open version, the "Targa" (below). With its five-speed gearbox, 160 bhp engine and ventilated disc brakes, one does not need to worry about using the maximum speed of around 225 kph (140 mph). It also makes it one of the fastest touring cars in the world. The bottom picture shows the men who helped in its development. They are (left to right): H. Metzger, P. Falk, F. Piëch (Chief of Experimental Department), H. Mimler, G. Endrich, H. Bott and Assistant Experimental Chief, A. Schneider.

1967

"GREEN LIGHT for the racing department" was the slogan for 1967. What we had seen for the second year running was to happen again to a hitherto unknown and unbelievable degree. Piëch and his men worked day and night. Large-scale finance, combined with careful planning and preparation, limited to a degree the glorious uncertainty of motoring sport a good while before the first starting flag fell. Now drivers were selected, and the experts were surprised when the Anglo/Irish crew, Vic Elford and David Stone, was nominated for the works rally team. The choice proved a good one, for they went on to win the Grand Touring car category of the European Rally Championship.

Our pictures show the two of them (left) in a bad snowstorm on the Col des Pennes during the German Rally, which they won; refuelling at St Sauveur (below) during the Monte Carlo Rally; and (bottom) after the victory celebration in front of the casino at Charbonnières.

WHAT MIGHT have been possible the previous year, given disciplined drivers, became an enthusiastically fêted reality in the 51st Targa Florio, for the Porsche 910 prototypes (two with 2.2 and two with 2.1 litre engines) scored a 1-2-3 victory and also took sixth place in this, the oldest road race in the world. However, the winners were not the favourites, but Porsche's "young men" Paul Hawkins (29 years old) and Rolf Stommelen (aged 24). The latter was also handed—as if to show the factory's appreciation—the second hill-climb Spyder for the eight qualifying events in the mountain championship as support to the reigning hill-climb champion, Gerhard Mitter.

In the first heat at Montseny, a 16.3 kilometres (10 miles) long winding mountain road north of Barcelona, this pleasant driver from the Rhineland left no doubt that he could justify the confidence placed in him. The playful ease with which he operated the lightweight (barely 1,200 lb) 240 bhp bolide up the mountain was splendid to watch (below) and gave rise to the conjecture, soon to be confirmed in events two, three and five (at Rossfeld, Mont Ventoux and Sestrière), that he could beat Mitter. At Monte Bondone his time up to a few kilometres before the finish, when he slid off due to mud left on the road by a tractor, was 3½ seconds better than Mitter, the future mountain champion, who also got into a slide at the same spot.

Our picture on the left shows a typical Targa Florio road section, visibly continued on the other side of the valley.

LONG-DISTANCE events hav
always been the forte of th
rear-engined Porsches from
Zuffenhausen. In 1967, howeve
they realised an old dream and wo
outright the 1,000 Kilometres o
the Nürburgring. They also too
second, third and fourth places an
against the 570 bhp 7 litre monste
from Texas, the Chapparal, whic
managed to lap the "Ring", despit
the new chicane, 10 seconds fast
than the quickest Porsche crew o
Siffert and Herrmann. There wa
just a slightly bitter after-taste t
this because the ADAC, the rac
organizers of this once-famou
event, manage to interest fewe
notable works teams and driver
each year.

The "Ring", just like th
Madonie "Targa", circuit shake
the very basis of any car, and is thu
feared by all works teams, althoug
these events are attractive an
challenging to the driver. Ford an
Ferrari think first of all of th
business that results from successe
and decide from this aspect. Whils
they enter one race meeting, the
shine by their absence from others
Only the little Porsches are every
where. In Sebring (USA) they wer
third and fourth behind the 3
times larger Fords; at Monza tw
P4s were followed by a Porsche i
third place, and in the tough, we
race at Spa Siffert/Herrman
followed the 5.7 litre Mirage For
into second place with their 2 litr
prototype.

Our pictures from top to botton
show first the start at Spa. On th
outside left, Porsche's most reliabl
man Jo Siffert goes into the left
hander. It is to him and Herrman
that Porsche entrust all experi
mental vehicles, such as the first 91
at Daytona. Siffert's speed plu
Herrmann's reliability are comple
mented by their exceptionally
sparing way of driving, which is o

estimable value to the men in the experimental department. The engines and transmissions of cars raced by these two drivers show by far the least wear, and the mechanics recognise this immediately. The middle picture is of the giant Udo Schütz in the winning car at the "Ring" and is an example of how exiguous is the construction of the cars. In its convertible form, even one as tall Schütz can be accommodated. Just! Bottom left is a Porsche discovery, the ex formula driver Kurt Ahrens, on the "jump" at Brünnchen.

The picture on this page shows the result of the winter development of 1966/67. It is the Le Mans 907 prototype, the first Porsche ever to exceed 300 kph (186 mph)

on the straight at Mulsanne. In this year's Le Mans 24 Hours, driven by Siffert/Herrmann, it scored the hat trick by taking the Index of Performance for the third time. Only 16 of the 55 starters reached the finish, five Porsches among them, a remarkably high percentage and renewed proof of the value given by Zuffenhausen in return for the purchaser's money.

Even a layman can see that this car is devoid of all that could adversely influence aerodynamics at high speed. There is no outside rear-view mirror; the fuel fillers are countersunk; and even the oil cooler intakes are no longer visible. All this, together with the vast "Phantom" screen—a name borrowed from the well-known faster-than-sound French fighter

aircraft—give this car an entirely new Porsche look. All nooks and crannies are absent—when air is needed, it is taken in at spots where it does not cost horsepower.

Comparisons, when based on the same six-cylinder over-240 bhp engine, look like this:

Carrera 6	267 kph (166 mph)
Long tailed Le Mans car 1966	276 kph (171 mph)
Le Mans Type 907	306 kph (190 mph)

This car began a development which promises to be most interesting and one which the old Professor Porsche was unfortunately no longer able to observe.

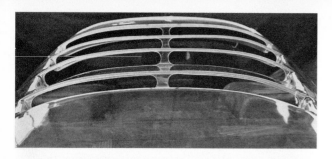

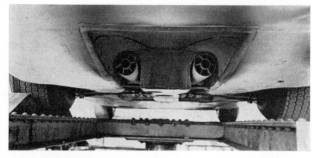

THE "STEPPED" rear window of the Le Mans type represented the result of a lot of experiment and many precise measurements. The elimination of the external rear-view mirror was only tolerated by the strict Le Mans organizers if the rear view of the driver, while stationary or at high speed, was quite unimpaired. This certainly was not the case at first, because the extremely thin and very elastic bodywork skin was subject to entirely different stresses when standing compared to when travelling at speed. The two pictures (top left) show the best compromise between loss of speed, angle of vision and stiffness.

The most significant point of this car is that it is low and "stretched", and those who want to look at the "Le Mans exhausts" must lie on the floor, for the increased length of the tail could not mean longer exhaust pipes, the length and diameter of which were accurately set to within half an inch. Apart from the six cylinder, Porsche also ran the eight cylinder fuel injection engine (below) in speed hill climbs.

THE TOP picture shows a time-keeping instrument developed by Porsche in conjunction with the Simplex company. With very few operatives, it can time accurately up to 10 vehicles in a 24-hour race, and show all individual times and pit stops. It can also compare the physical ability of the drivers, and in this respect the instrument provided interesting information which, until then, could only be guessed at but not proven.

It showed up the so-called "sprinters", with their vaccillating up-and-down performances, clearly differing from the "constant" drivers who, during a 24-hour race, hardly displayed any differences in their lap times. Quite unintentionally, the instrument proved the correctness of the decision to entrust the latter type of driver with new developments.

The engine and transmission specialists have always said that "sprinter" transmissions showed far more wear compared to those of "constant" drivers, which is the reason why "constant" drivers are so much in demand and liked by experimental engineers.

Not only are the cars looked after, but also those who drive and maintain them. The layman only has a vague idea of what is required to keep all the men fed, and the necessary items (bottom picture) cannot quickly be bought behind the pits during the race! In Porsche's case they are pre-cooked and transported in Thermos flasks from the village of Teloché to the pits, eight miles away. Here we see (top right) the wife of the Chief of the Experimental Department, Piëch (background), a mother of four

children, with her landlady Mme Boulard in the process of preparing a considerable quantity of the very popular goulash soup.

1968

OVERALL VICTORY, almost certain in the 1967 Monte Carlo Rally up until literally the last minutes, became a fact for Porsche in 1968 when Vic Elford and David Stone (left) inscribed the 911S Porsche on the long list of winners of this famous winter rally. The Porsche works must be grateful to Huschke von Hanstein for having "bought" these two outstanding drivers. The fact that they were world class had taken time to prove itself and was due to the fact that they drove vehicles which were not as tough as their drivers.

"Let's not talk about the long run to Monaco, which is unnecessary, it's the big final loop that has to be watched," said Vic, "but very hard driving will be needed on the last night and we rely on one another blindly. But the whole—as so often before—would be a fairly uncertain thing if we did not have such a well developed and tough car. One can't do anything else except win with it." Our picture on the previous page—taken during the last night on the special stage of the Turini—underlines Elford's words. David, in his safety harness, microphone close to his lips, reads from the "bible" like a good uncle sitting by the fireside. Vic is all eyes and ears, and after half the night was over both knew that they had triumphed over all those who, a few hours previously, could have been a danger to them. But one Porsche was not enough: the Finnish pair, Toivonen/Tiukkanen (below), got another Porsche into second place overall.

The third man, BMC rally ace Rauno Aaltonen, said resignedly at the quayside in Monaco: "If I'd had another 100 bhp, I could have competed". Pictured right are the cheerful victors, Elford (left) and Stone.

PORSCHE'S persistent battle to maintain and enlarge their North American sales has never had a bigger nor, for the salesmen, more lasting fillip than at the beginning of the 1968 motor sporting season at the "American Le Mans"—the Daytona 24-hour race. There, the three 2.2 litre fuel injection 8 cylinder prototypes trounced the opposition and, in icy cold but dry and sunny weather, the winning car finished no less than 44 laps ahead of the fourth-place car on this short 4¼-mile circuit and the three Porsches crossed the finishing line in formation (bottom right). Of 65 starters, 25 finished, 11 of them Porsches, and even for the Americans, fed on superlatives, this was a sensation. In all probability the final result could have looked even better for the works if the oyster shells, thrown from the in-field on to the track itself, had not caused 26 burst tyres. Mitter's car had an accident as a result of a blown tyre, but fortunately without serious consequences.

The opposition—apart from the red Alfas, which could not keep up right from the start but which lasted the 24 hours—was altogether twice as powerful, and included the Howmet turbine and the Ford GT40s driven by Ickx/Redman and Hawkins/Hobbs, and also a British Lola. In 1967 the 4 litre Ferraris had covered 666 laps in the 24 hours, a total of 2,537 miles. This year the winning 2.2 litre Porsche covered 673 laps, some 2,564 miles. Vic Elford was particularly noteworthy because until then his name had been made only in rallies (he had just won the Monte for Porsche). Together with his team mates Neerpasch, Stommelen, Herrmann and Siffert he had a seat in the Daytona-winning car, while Siffert and Herrmann also crewed the second-place Porsche

(above)! Thus began for him a new chapter and if appearances do not deceive, the world will certainly hear a lot more of this cheerful but unbelievably tenacious and strong-willed Britisher. Whenever they see him, a Gauloise in one hand and a cup of strong tea in the other, those hoping to take up the cudgels with him should know that this dark-haired character can virtually achieve the impossible at the wheel.

PORSCHE could hardly be said to lack a successful competition history—yet never were they as richly rewarded as in the first three months of 1968. In rallies their cars collected outright wins in the Monte Carlo, Swedish, San Remo and Hessen events. In the touring car category they filled the first four places in the 4 hours of Monza. And in the international championship for makes they had a threefold triumph at Daytona and, a mere six weeks later, in the second round of the championship, the 12 hours of Sebring, they also finished with a 1–2 victory. For the 15th time the 30-strong Porsche racing team crossed the Atlantic in the direction of Miami Beach, to do battle at nearby Sebring with the brand-new 5 litre Lola-Chevrolets, the Howmet turbine car, the Camaro-Chevrolets, Ford GTs, and the 3 litre Alpine prototype. Four works Porsche prototypes with short tails, fitted with 2.2 litre 8 cylinder fuel injection engines which had been used successfully at Daytona, were lined up against this field of bigger-engined cars.

The 60,000 spectators got their money's worth and of the entry of 69 cars half kept running on the 5 mile circuit. There were spin-outs, collisions and many mechanical failures, as in all long-distance races, and the two works cars driven by Scarfiotti/ Buzzetta and Mitter/Stommelen also succumbed. For 11 of the 12 hours the ultimate victors Herrmann/Siffert led the field, a Lola having led for a short while at the start. The battle between the Ford GT40 of Hawkins/Hobbs and the Anglo-German team of Elford/Neerpasch was decided in favour of the Porsche and a double victory was in the bag. Our three pictures show the winning car (49) making a good start, cornering in the sunshine, and undergoing a driver change during a night-time pit stop.

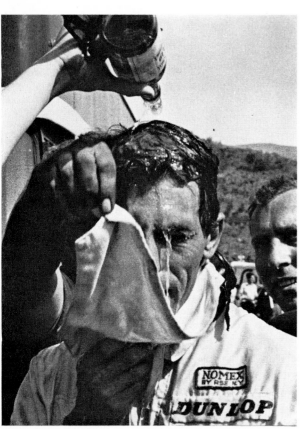

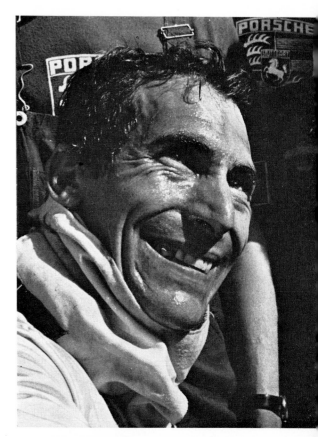

COMPARISONS are odious, but we shall never-theless attempt this one, after what took place at the 1968 Targa Florio in Sicily. This, the 52nd of the series, was one man's race—Vic Elford's (left). His physical achievement alone—the scirocco wind had been unduly high for days—his driving ability, his courage and his unshakeable determination to win, despite losing 18 minutes through no fault of his own, permit comparisons with the great ones like Nuvolari and Fangio. When he handed the car to Umberto Maglioli after four laps and was barely able to stand, his wife said: "I've never seen Vic like this in my life!" When they showed him the chequered flag, he drove the car into the remotest corner of the *parc ferme* and we were among the handful of people to see him get out of the car after that incredible drive. Then and there originated a series of Elford portraits (bottom) which are some of the most impressive in my life as a photographer. Within a few seconds the contents of three big Pellegrino bottles disappeared over his head and down his sweat-stained overalls. Two cigarettes dropped from his hands before he managed to light a third. Exhaustion, happiness and pleasure marked his per-spiring face, and when he saw his wife among the people there was no holding him back. The Italians, still hoping for an Alfa win up to the last moment, forgot their nationalistic feelings and frantically yelled their approval: Elford! Elford!

What had happened in that last hour of this race-in-the-heat can best be summarized in the words of Porsche driver, Karl Freiherr von Wendt, who had taken part in this event for the first time and won his class: "I felt as if I was burning up inside when I found a last slice of lemon in my pocket. When I got it between my teeth, I thought I was under a cold shower. Never have I taken anything more refreshing in my life". Von Wendt is pictured in his Carrera 6 (above).

223

THE NURBURGRING 1,000 Kilometres is Porsche's home round of the international championship, and they were therefore delighted with the 1967 result when the cars scored a resounding "blanket" victory. For 1968 two of the new 3 litre 8 cylinder machines were taken along to spearhead the white cars' attack, backed up by another pair of the well-proven and extremely successful 2.2 litre vehicles.

The 3 litre car driven by Jo Siffert and Vic Elford took the lead at the start of the second lap, after the Swiss driver had made a superb Le Mans-type start. They then held the lead, apart from pit stops, throughout the 44 lap, 6-hour race. Opposition came from the 4.7 litre Ford GT40s of Ickx/Hawkins, Redman/Hobbs, and from the blood-red Alfa Romeos, but neither could sustain the pace set by the leading Porsche. Ickx was very quick indeed in his Ford, but poor Hawkins could not match his speed that day and the car dropped away from the 3 litre Porsche.

Mitter and Scarfiotti in the second 3 litre led for the first lap and then slipped into second place behind Siffert/Elford. But the car began to behave strangely, and after many stops was retired with a suspected chassis breakage. The two smaller cars,

driven by Herrmann/Stommelen and Neerpasch/Buzzetta ran faultlessly throughout, often taking the leading two places when their big sister stopped for fuel and driver changes, and finally finished second and fourth overall. Hard driving by Ickx pushed the Gulf Ford into third place.

The home team of Bitter/Joest were winners of the 2 litre Group 4 class with their private Carrera 6, with the similar car of Von Wendt/Kaussen second and a British Chevron third.

The photographs show Siffert leaping his car over one of the Nürburgring's notorious humps, and about to lap the second-in-class Carrera 6 of Von Wendt and Willi Kaussen. Brushing close against the overhanging undergrowth is the handsome little 2 litre type 910 of privateers Huhn and Dechent. Private entrants helped greatly in making this race another Porsche success, no less than 17 of the cars finishing in the first 35!

Finally, below, is a shot of Mitter in the latest lightweight hill-climb car, winning the tragic Rossfeld event in which Scarfiotti lost his life, and Stommelen was injured. Mitter went on to clinch his second consecutive hill-climb title.

From the old "aluminium box to plastic bodywork

29 years of constructing sports racing cars

THE PREDECESSOR of all Porsches is this 1939 sports car (left) built by the Porsche design office at the instigation of Hühnlein; it was to be used in a non-stop run from Berlin to Rome. The start of the Second World War prevented this, but the car survived the war in Austria and, driven by the one-armed Otto Mathé, scored notable successes, including winning the Alpine Cup. It consisted of a normal VW chassis and engine, plus a Roots-type blower, and the air resistance coefficient of its aluminium body was lower than that of the type 356.

The roadster above was built by Ferry Porsche in 1948. It had a 1,131 cc VW engine and was, in fact, the first "real" Porsche. It wandered from Austria to Switzerland and finally Germany, where it is now the proudest exhibit of the little works museum at Porsche. Like the later Spyder types, this one had the engine in front of the rear axle. There was a multi-tube frame under the aluminium skin, and the car weighed only 596 kilograms, (about 11¾ cwt). Until a few years ago, it was often seen at the International Porsche rallies.

THE CAR below is the first Porsche in its original form, with a long engine cover on which one can just see the air entry slots on the left and right. First exhibited in the spring of 1949 at Geneva, the type 356 (right) became the biggest-selling Porsche, and its slogan was: "driving in its most beautiful form". Three of these entirely hand-built cars laid the foundation of Porsche's sporting reputation after the second World War. Their aluminium bodies soon gave rise to the nickname "Ali-box" and they were built in Gmünd (Carinthia-Austria). In the autumn of 1951, one of them set up a distance record at the Monthléry track, near Paris, of 10,968 kilometres (6,811 miles) in 72 hours, an average of 94.7 mph (old record 90.41 mph). They also won at Le Mans, the never-to-be-forgotten Mille Miglia, the road marathon that is now also history (the Liège-Rome-Liège), and the Coupe des Alpes, too. The series of wins of one of these vehicles, which was modernised time after time, reached well into the sixties, and it is also now in the works museum. The car shown belonged, after King Farouk's fall, to the Regent of Egypt of those days—Prince Abdel-Moneim in Heliopolis. Our bottom right picture shows the aerodynamically improved car by the Frankfurt coachbuilders Weidenhausen. It had the pushrod engine and gained a double class victory at Le Mans in 1953, driven by Glöckler/Herrmann and Frankenberg/Frère. This so-called Le Mans Coupé was the predecessor of the type 550. It had 80 bhp, a maximum speed of over 125 mph, and weighed just under 11 cwt.

IN 1953, the newest of the successful type 550 appeared—the so-called "hump-backed" car which was widely exhibited. It had a wide head-fairing behind its two comfortable seats, and it was that which gave it its nickname. The four-camshaft engine produced 110 bhp at 7000 rpm, which gave the car a maximum speed of 225 kph (140 mph), and in 1954/55 it became known as the "Spyder" for the first time. The works cars were provided with differently painted tails, to aid recognition from the pits. Hans Herrmann's particularly famous "red-tail" car (no 41) went from victory to victory. Seventy-five replicas of the original type 550 with enclosed passenger seat, (top left, opposite page), were built up until 1957. A one-off prototype was the 1957 super-light design called "Micky

Mouse" (top right, opposite page) which, with Richard von Frankenberg at the helm, was written off that same year at the Avus. The very small frontal area made it particularly aerodynamic. Interesting also was the surface oil cooler and the welded magnesium body "skin", used for the first time. Its poisonous white fire in the Frankenberg accident will forever remain in the author's memory. A further experimental version appeared in 1957 in practice for the 1,000 Kilometres of the Nürburgring. This one was five inches lower than the RS Spyder, had no air intakes in front, and its oil cooling was under the front bonnet, which was double skinned. The cars numbered 22 and 21 clearly show these differences; the driver was Maglioli (bottom right).

ON THE far left we show three variations of the type 550A. Special recognition features were: 1.5 litre engine, compression ratio 9.8:1, 135 bhp, maximum speed 150 mph. For the first time, Porsche peg steering replaced the VW unit, and the bodybuilders were Wendler of Reutlingen. These types were very successful in the hands of Jean Behra and Count Wolfgang von Trips. The type 718, also known as the RSK, (pictured, bottom, on the facing page) could reach 155 mph with its 148 bhp at 8,000 rpm. This prototype, developed from the 1957 Spyder and made into a central-seater vehicle (left), was entered for Formula 2 events and Behra won with it from Stirling Moss at Rheims. After the first successful attempts with this car, Porsche made its debut at Monte Carlo in 1959 in a World Championship *grande epreuve*. However, this vehicle (below) crashed on the first lap, driven by von Trips. In 1960, four improved cars followed, and Stirling Moss had the first (bottom two pictures).

HERE in the development department (No 1 Works), where the RS60s were built and where engine assembly can be seen in the foreground (left), each of the qualified mechanics looked after his individual engine until its test-bed run—just as it was at the beginning of series production in 1950. Note that the walls had long become too small for the countless mementoes from all over the world. Above is shown the wooden former for the aluminium body, which was constantly being filed and chopped about at the well-known Wendler workshops in Reutlingen.

THESE RS61s do not come from a production line as it would appear here. They are the end products of a dozen or so selected specialist craftsmen who, with care and after many years experience, assemble each vehicle piece by piece. They are the same mechanics who, here and on the other side of the Atlantic, wherever "their" cars join the fray, win or lose, quietly and modestly give of their very best, to the last ounce. Only some of them from those past years are mentioned here: the chassis specialist "Papa" Enz; transmission expert Huber; the small, cynical but perfectionist engine-man Enz; "Luck" Lehner, the wiring and electrical specialist; engine experts Alber and Dubies, the latter also known as "Monsieur Dubois"; "Mister" Dietrich, the chassis measurement specialist; "Bims" Lehner; and Ackermann and Vogel, both chassis mechanics. Without them, their endless idealism and professional pride, their very high craftsmanship, conscientiousness, smiles and curses, this book would not have been produced.

THESE GP machines—born from Formula 2 cars—involved Porsche in the merciless and equally expensive Formula 1 battle. As was to be expected, their rivals, with wits sharpened by many years of experience, forced Porsche to show ultra rapid and extreme adaptability, and within a few months new types appeared. There was the carburettor-engined car (top left) first seen at Syracuse and driven by Dan Gurney; then the fuel-injection experimental machine (using the Schäfer system) driven by Bonnier in Monte Carlo (bottom left). Top right is shown a simple variation with axial blower cooling and Bosch fuel injection which came to grief in Holland, driven by Ben Pon. The Formula 1 non-plus-ultra Porsche, with the eight cylinder carburettor engine and disc brakes (bottom right), overcame the styling mistakes of the past, and looked as if it truly belonged to the Grand Prix field created by the British and Italians. The year of its debut— it won the World Championship event at Rouen—was also its swan song, but the eight cylinder engine was destined for big things in the future.

THE PLASTIC era at the Porsche works began with the 2 litre Carrera GTS 904. Within a few months, more than 100 examples of this glass-fibre bodied machine were made by outside contractors but (and this was something quite new) they were not assembled by the racing shop but were completely finished where they had been built. There was, and still is, a spare parts catalogue for this vehicle, and items can be ordered over-the-counter. The proven four camshaft engine, which many thought old-fashioned and something of a museum piece, gives this 180 bhp vehicle a top speed of about 165 mph. Its advantages are robustness and reliability and, despite weighing 14¾ cwt, it gained a double victory on its first attempt in the Targa Florio and many other successes followed.

THE box-section body of the 904, the top part of which is so light that it can be held up by a couple of girls, only obtains its stiffness—a pre-requisite for good road-holding—by being joined to the lower half of the chassis. The construction shows—when lit from inside—the limited number of stiffening and "welding" ribs, which are invisible after the car is painted. The system shown here gave rise to the slogan "cars from the spraygun". The worker using a face mask operates a three-way gun to make a boot lid: the outside jets spray synthetic resin into the mould while the large central jet emits chopped-up glass fibre, and the material then hardens in the mould. This glass fibre laminate can easily be sawn, sanded and polished. The same applies to repairs—one does not "beat out" panels any more. Just like rubber-patching a bicycle tyre, there is a portable kit in the car which enables small repairs to be carried out quite easily. The night-time shot of the cockpit shows the simple and clear lines, with everything arranged for sporting motoring. Comfort is of lesser importance than function-alism.

THE SUCCESSOR to the 904 was the Carrera 6, which also has plastic bodywork, but made differently from its predecessor. The exceptionally low construction—only the wheels necessitate a higher outline—seems fascinatingly outlandish due to its crouching animal-like form. Against the Targa Florio "ugly duckling", this ultra-flat vehicle can best be likened to a flounder, and no Porsche-bodied racing machine has ever summarized such a number of functional characteristics. None could so shock or inspire enthusiasm, and whenever bystanders have a chance of seeing one, large crowds form. Its very much lightened plastic body surrounds a multi-tube frame which carries the engine and suspension. The engine has been developed from the 911 six cylinder—hence Carrera 6—which develops 210 bhp at 8,000 rpm. The weight is about 12 cwt, and maximum speed around 175 mph. Pages 190-203 show the brief but steeply rising career of this instantly successful vehicle. Its protagonists are those young men who, following the old Professor Porsche, now form the third generation in the works, and of whom he would indeed be proud were he still among us.

THE CARRERA 6 has the most unusual "face" ever given to a Porsche by its designers and stylists. What has become of the crude "shark's mouth" look of the 'fifties which, admired by all, was presented to the super critical scrutineers in Brescia prior to the last Mille Miglia? Where are the many other types which we admired and respected whenever they appeared from under their protective tarpaulins? No doubt about it, this car only has the name Porsche in common with the vehicles of those earlier years. The "nostrils" of the brake cooling ducts are now below the "maw", contrary to previous arrangements, and oil cooling is within the "luggage" lid due to aerodynamic considerations. All is so neat and low that getting in requires gull-wing doors, while holes were also fashioned into the body—where none had been previously—to cool the rear brakes and transmission. One seems to be—at least so it appears to us—near the end of this development. For if the lessons learnt in racing are to benefit series production cars—and this factor is always emphasized—then the designers of such vehicles must be set tasks which point to future trends. That they have always managed to cope with the problems facing them is amply proven by the past decades of motoring sport.

THESE TWO pages are dedicated to the 910, the 1967 prototype used for the first time in the critical glare of publicity at the Monte Bondone round of the Mountain Championship, driven by Hans Herrmann (bottom left). Lighter and lower again than its predecessor, it has 13 inch cast elektron centre-lock wheels, developed by Porsche, and the eight cylinder fuel-injection engine (above). Although engine output and performance data were on the secret list, it was clear that for the experimental depart-ment these were already yesterday's figures. Their cares are for the future prototypes, and may we express the wish that they will be yet further landmarks for the small and courageous works. Nothing can endanger this company, so long as designers and workers put quality before quantity, and their products continue to purvey pleasure and relaxation to those who remain in-dividualists, despite all attempts at standard-isation. There will be people like that until the end of our days.

AROUND the New Year of 1966/67 there was a little festivity like the one on March 21, 1951 when the 500th car left the works. This time it was for the 100,000th Porsche—a Targa model, decorated with mimosa and here looked after by the competent and attractive press chief of Porsche, Evi Butz. The car was destined for the Württemberg county police. If the now somewhat forgotten slogan "driving in its pleasantest form" has ever been justified, then this is the car that creates constantly increasing interest and its owners more than ever form a circle of motorists who stick out head and shoulders above the car-buying millions. And as long as there are people like that, there will be motor manufacturers like Porsche.

YEAR	MODEL DESIG.	No. of CYLS.	STROKE/BORE	CAPA-CITY	COMP. RATIO	BHP @ RPM DIN	SAE	No. of GEARS	WHEEL-BASE	LENGTH	WIDTH	HEIGHT	WEIGHT (lbs)
1950	356/1100	4	64/73·5	1,086	7:1	40/4,200		4+R	$82\frac{11}{16}$	$155\frac{9}{16}$	$65\frac{3}{8}$	$51\frac{3}{16}$ (Coupé / Cabriolet)	1,829 (Coupé / Cabriolet)
1951	356/1100	4	64/73·5	7:1	7:1	40/4,200		4+R	"	"	"	"	"
	356/1300	4	64/80	1,286	6·5:1	44/4,200	50/4,500	4+R	"	"	"	"	"
From Oct.	356/1500	4	74/80	1,488	7:1	60/5,000	70/4,800	4+R	"	"	"	"	"
1952	356/1100	4	64/73·5	1,086	7:1	40/4,200		4+R	"	"	"	"	"
	356/1300	4	64/80	1,286	6·5:1	44/4,200	50/4,500	4+R	"	"	"	"	"
Till Sept.	356/1500	4	74/80	1,488	7:1	60/5,000	70/4,800	4+R	"	"	"	"	"
From Sept.	356/1500	4	74/80	1,488	7:1	55/4,400	64/4,800	4+R	"	"	"	"	"
From Oct.	356/1500S	4	74/80	1,488	8·2:1	70/5,000	82/5,400	4+R	"	"	"	"	"
1953	356/1100	4	64/73·5	1,086	7:1	40/4,200		4+R	"	"	"	"	"
	356/1300	4	64/80	1,286	6·5:1	44/4,200	50/4,500	4+R	"	"	"	"	"
	356/1500	4	74/80	1,488	7:1	55/4,400	64/4,800	4+R	"	"	"	"	"
	356/1500S	4	74/80	1,488	8·2:1	70/5,000	82/5,400	4+R	"	"	"	"	"
From Nov.	356/1300S	4	74/74·5	1,290	8·2:1	60/5,500	71/5,700	4+R	"	"	"	"	"
1954	356/1100	4	64/73·5	1,086	7:1	40/4,200		4+R	"	"	"	$51\frac{3}{16}$ (Coupé / Cabriolet) $47\frac{7}{8}$ (Speedster)	1,676·5 (Speedster) Coupé/Cab unchanged
Till May	356/1300	4	64/80	1,286	6·5:1	44/4,200	50/4,500	4+R	"	"	"	"	"
	356/1300S	4	74/74·5	1,290	8·2:1	60/5,500	71/5,700	4+R	"	"	"	"	"
June to Nov.	356/1300A	4	74/74·5	1,290	6·5:1	44/4,200	50/4,500	4+R	"	"	"	"	"
Till Nov.	356/1500	4	74/80	1,488	7:1	55/4,400	64/4,800	4+R	"	"	"	"	"
Till Nov.	356/1500S	4	74/80	1,488	8·2:1	70/5,000	82/5,400	4+R	"	"	"	"	"
From Nov.	356/1300	4	74/74·5	1,290	6·5:1	44/4,200	50/4,500	4+R	"	"	"	"	"
From Nov.	356/1300S	4	74/74·5	1,290	7·5:1	60/5,500	71/5,700	4+R	"	"	"	"	"
From Nov.	356/1500	4	74/80	1,488	7:1	55/4,400	64/4,800	4+R	"	"	"	"	"
From Nov.	356/1500S	4	74/80	1,488	8·2:1	70/5,000	82/5,400	4+R	"	"	"	"	"
1955 Till Oct.	356/1300	4	74/74·5	1,290	6·5:1	44/4,200	50/4,500	4+R	"	"	"	"	"
	356/1300S	4	74/74·5	1,290	7·5:1	60/5,500	71/5,700	4+R	"	"	"	"	"
	356/1500	4	74/80	1,488	7:1	55/4,400	64/4,800	4+R	"	"	"	"	"
	356/1500S	4	74/80	1,488	8·2:1	70/5,000	82/5,400	4+R	"	"	"	"	"
From Oct. (1956 models)	356A/1300	4	74/74·5	1,290	6·5:1	44/4,200	50/4,500	4+R	"	"	$65\frac{3}{4}$	$51\frac{1}{16}$ (Coupé / Cabriolet) $47\frac{7}{8}$ (Speedster) $50\frac{13}{16}$ (Hardtop)	1,873·9 (Coupé / Cabriolet) 1,676·5 (Speedster) 1,873·9 (Hardtop)
	356A/1300S	4	74/74·5	1,290	7·5:1	60/5,500	71/5,700	4+R	"	"	"	"	"
	356A/1600	4	74/82·5	1,582	7·5:1	60/4,500	70/4,500	4+R	"	"	"	"	"
	356A/1600S	4	74/82·5	1,582	8·5:1	75/5,000	88/5,000	4+R	"	"	"	"	"

YEAR	MODEL DESIG.	No. of CYLS.	STROKE/BORE	CAPACITY	COMP. RATIO	BHP @ RPM DIN	SAE	No. of GEARS	WHEEL-BASE	LENGTH WIDTH HEIGHT (all these dimensions in inches)	WEIGHT (lbs)
1956	356A/1300	4	74/74·5	1,290	6·5:1	44/4,200	50/4,500	4+R			
	356A/1300S	4	74/74·5	1,290	7·5:1	60/5,500	71/5,700	4+R			,,
	356A/1600	4	74/82·5	1,582	7·5:1	60/4,500	70/4,500	4+R			,,
	356A/1600S	4	74/82·5	1,582	8·5:1	75/5,000	88/5,000	4+R			,,
1957 Till Sept	356A/1300	4	74/74·5	1,290	6·5:1	44/4,200	50/4,500	4+R			,,
	356A/1300S	4	74/74·5	1,290	7·5:1	60/5,500	71/5,700	4+R			,,
	356A/1600	4	74/82·5	1,582	7·5:1	60/4,500	70/4,500	4+R			,,
	356A/1600S	4	74/82·5	1,582	8·5:1	75/5,000	88/5,000	4+R			,,
From Sept. carb. change	356A/1600	4	74/82·5	1,582	7·5:1	60/4,500	70/4,500	4+R			,,
	356A/1600S	4	74/82·5	1,582	8·5:1	75/5,000	88/5,000	4+R			,,
1958	356A/1600	4	74/82·5	1,582	7·5:1	60/4,500	70/4,500	4+R			,,
	356A/1600S	4	74/82·5	1,582	8·5:1	75/5,000	88/5,000	4+R			,,
1959 Till Sept.	356A/1600	4	74/82·5	1,582	7·5:1	60/4,500	70/4,500	4+R			,,
	356A/1600S	4	74/82·5	1,582	8·5:1	75/5,000	88/5,000	4+R			,,
From Sept.	356B/1600	4	74/82·5	1,582	7·5:1	60/4,500	70/4,500	4+R	157$\frac{7}{8}$	$52\frac{7}{16}$ (Coupé Cabriolet) · $51\frac{9}{16}$ (Roadster)	1,984·1 (Coupé, Cabriolet, Karmann Hardtop) 1,918 (Roadster)
	356B/1600S	4	74/82·5	1,582	8·5:1	75/5,000	88/5,000	4+R	,,	,,	,,
1960	356B/1600	4	74/82·5	1,582	7·5:1	60/4,500	70/4,500	4+R			,,
	356B/1600S	4	74/82·5	1,582	8·5:1	75/5,000	88/5,000	4+R			,,
	356B/1600-S90	4	74/82·5	1,582	9:1	90/5,500	102/5,500	4+R			,,
1961 Till Sept.	356B/1600	4	74/82·5	1,582	7·5:1	60/4,500	70/4,500	4+R			,,
	356B/1600S	4	74/82·5	1,582	8·5:1	75/5,000	88/5,000	4+R		($52\frac{7}{16}$ Karmann Hardtop intro'd)	,,
	356B/1600-S90	4	74/82·5	1,582	9:1	90/5,500	102/5,500	4+R			,,
From Sept. 1962 models	356B/1600	4	74/82·5	1,582	7·5:1	60/4,500	70/4,500	4+R			,,
	356B/1600S	4	74/82·5	1,582	8·5:1	75/5,000	88/5,000	4+R			,,
	356B/1600-S90	4	74/82·5	1,582	9:1	90/5,500	102/5,500	4+R			,,
1962 Till July	356B/1600	4	74/82·5	1,582	7·5:1	60/4,500	70/4,500	4+R			,,
	356B/1600S	4	74/82·5	1,582	8·5:1	75/5,000	88/5,000	4+R			,,
	356B/1600-S90	4	74/82·5	1,582	9:1	90/5,500	102/5,500	4+R		($51\frac{3}{4}$ GT Carrera Coupé intro'd)	,,
From July 1963 models	356B/1600	4	74/82·5	1,582	7·5:1	60/4,500	70/4,500	4+R			,,
	356B/1600S	4	74/82·5	1,582	8·5:1	75/5,000	88/5,000	4+R			,,
	356B/1600-S90	4	74/82·5	1,582	9:1	90/5,500	102/5,500	4+R			,,

YEAR	MODEL DESIG.	No. of CYLS.	STROKE/BORE	CAPA-CITY	COMP. RATIO	BHP @ RPM DIN	BHP @ RPM SAE	No. of GEARS	WHEEL-BASE	LENGTH	WIDTH	HEIGHT	WEIGHT (lbs)
1963 Till July	356B/1600	4	74/82.5	1,582	7.5:1	60/4,500	70/4,500	4+R	,,	,,	,,	,,	,,
	356B/1600S	4	74/82.5	1,582	8.5:1	75/5,000	88/5,000	4+R	,,	,,	,,	,,	,,
	356B/1600-S90	4	74/82.5	1,582	9:1	90/5,500	102/5,500	4+R	,,	,,	,,	,,	,,
From July	356C/1600C	4	74/82.5	1,582	8.5:1	75/5,200	88/5,200	4+R	,,	,,	,,	$51\frac{7}{8}$	2,039.2
	356C/1600SC	4	74/82.5	1,582	9.5:1	95/5,800	107/5,800	4+R	,,	,,	,,	,,	,,
1964	356C/1600C	4	74/82.5	1,582	8.5:1	75/5,200	88/5,200	4+R	,,	,,	,,	,,	,,
	356C/1600SC	4	74/82.5	1,582	9.5:1	95/5,800	107/5,800	4+R	,,	,,	,,	,,	,,
From Sept. 1965 model	911 de Luxe	6	80/66	1,991	9:1	130/6,100	148/6,100	5+R	87	164	63.4	52	2,376
1965	356C/1600C	4	74/82.5	1,582	8.5:1	75/5,200	88/5,200	4+R	$82\frac{11}{16}$	$157\frac{7}{8}$	$65\frac{3}{4}$	$51\frac{7}{8}$	2,039.2
	356C/1600SC	4	74/82.5	1,582	9.5:1	95/5,800	107/5,800	4+R	,,	,,	,,	,,	,,
From May	911 de Luxe	6	66/80	1,991	9:1	130/6,100	148/6,100	5+R	87	164	63.4	52	2,376
	912	4	74/82.5	1,582	9.3:1	90/5,800	102/5,800	4+R	,,	,,	,,	,,	2,134
1966 Till Sept.	912	4	74/82.5	1,582	9.3:1	90/5,800	102/5,800	4+R	,,	,,	,,	,,	2,134
	911 de Luxe	6	66/80	1,991	9:1	130/6,100	148/6,100	5+R	,,	,,	,,	,,	2,376
From Sept. 1967 models	911N	6	66/80	1,991	9:1	130/6,100	148/6,100	5+R	,,	,,	,,	,,	,,
	911S	6	66/80	1,991	9.8:1	160/6,600	180/6,600	5+R	,,	,,	,,	,,	2,270
1967 Till Sept.	912	4	74/82.5	1,582	9.3:1	90/5,800	102/5,800	4+R	,,	,,	,,	,,	2,134
	911N	6	66/80	1,991	9:1	130/6,100	148/6,100	5+R	,,	,,	,,	,,	2,376
	911S	6	66/80	1,991	9.8:1	160/6,600	180/6,600	5+R	,,	,,	,,	,,	2,270
From Sept.	911L	6	66/80	1,991	9:1	130/6,100	148/6,100	5+R	,,	,,	,,	,,	2,384
	911T	6	66/80	1,991	8.6:1	110/5,800	125/5,800	4+R	,,	,,	,,	,,	,,

RECENT COMPETITION MODELS

YEAR	MODEL DESIG.	No. of CYLS.	STROKE/BORE	CAPA-CITY	COMP. RATIO	BHP @ RPM DIN	No. of GEARS	WHEEL-BASE	LENGTH	WIDTH	HEIGHT	WEIGHT (lbs)
1964	904GTS	4	74/92	1,966	9.8:1	180/7,000	5+R	$90\frac{9}{16}$	$161\frac{1}{16}$	$60\frac{5}{8}$	$42\frac{5}{16}$	1,432.9
1967	910/6	6	66/80	1,991	10.3:1	220/8,000	5+R	,,	$161\frac{15}{16}$	$66\frac{1}{8}$	$38\frac{9}{16}$	1,267.6
	910/8	8	54/80	2,195	10.2:1	270/8,600	5+R	,,	,,	,,	,,	1,322.7
	910 Berg	8	54.6/76	1,981	10.4:1	272/9,000	5+R	,,	152	$67\frac{5}{16}$	$30\frac{1}{8}$	992
	907 Langheck	6	66/80	1,991	10.3:1	220/8,000	5+R	,,	$183\frac{1}{8}$	,,	,,	1,300.7
	911R	6	66/80	1,991	10.3:1	210/8,000	5+R	$86\frac{11}{16}$	$163\frac{5}{16}$	$63\frac{3}{8}$	$50\frac{3}{8}$	1,763.7
1968	907/8	8	54.6/80	2,195	10.2:1	270/8,600	5+R	$90\frac{9}{16}$	$158\frac{13}{16}$	$67\frac{3}{4}$	37	1,322.7
	907/6	6	66/80	1,991	10.3:1	220/8,000	5+R	,,	$158\frac{13}{16}$	,,	,,	1,267.6
	Carrera 6 (906)	6	66/80	1,991	10.3:1	210/8,000	5+R	,,	,,	,,	,,	,,

Major Porsche Competition Victories 1953–1968

EVENT	CLASS	DRIVER/CREW
1953		
Monaco sports cars	1500 cc	Neumann
4th Sestriere Rally	1500 cc Sports	Polenski/Martinengo
Mille Miglia	1300 cc Prod Sports	von Hoesch/Engel
	1500 cc Prod Sports	Herrmann/Bauer
Hyeres 12-Hours	1500 cc	Olivier/Veuillet
	1100 cc	Hampel/Molinelli
Le Mans 24-Hours	1500 cc Sports	von Frankenberg/Frere—Glockler/Herrmann equal 1st
Roubaix Grand Prix	Overall	Olivier
AVUS races	1100 cc	Trenkel
German GP sports	1100 cc Sports	Trenkel
	1500 cc Sports	Herrmann
Schauinsland Hill Climb	1500 cc	Herrmann
Nürburg 1,000 Kms	1500 cc Sports	Trenkel/Schluter
	1300 cc Prod Sports	von Hoesch/Engel
Carrera Panamericana	1600 cc	Herrarte
1954		
Buenos Aires 1,000 Kms	1500 cc Sports	Juhan/Asturias
Buenos Aires 1,000 Miles	Sports	Mayol/Gobbi
Tulip Rally	1600 cc	Engel/Armbrecht
Mille Miglia	1600 cc	von Frankenberg/Sauter
	1500 cc Sports	Herrmann/Linge
Acropolis Rally	Overall	Maleric/Cerne
Le Mans 24-Hours	1500 cc	Claes/Stasse
	1100 cc	Duntov/Oliver
Porto Grand Prix	1500 cc	Martorel
Reims 12-Hours	Sports	Polenski/von Frankenberg
Swiss Mountain GP	1500 cc Sports	Stanek
	1100 cc Sports	von Hanstein
	Racing Cars	Mathe
European GP Nurburg	Racing Cars	Herrmann
Tour de France	Sports	Storez/Linge
AVUS races	Sports	von Frankenberg
	1600 cc GT	Polenski
Gaisberg Hill-Climb	Sports	Mathe
Geneva Rally	1600 cc	Kienle/Wutherich
Bahamas Speed Week:		
Nassau Sports race	Overall & 1500 SP	von Hanstein
Bahama AC race	Overall & 1500 SP	von Hanstein
Nassau Trophy	Overall & 1500 SP	von Hanstein
1955		
Buenos Aires 1,000 Kms	1500 cc	Juhan/Sales Chaves
Sebring 12-Hours	1600 cc Prod	von Hanstein/Linge
	1300 cc Sports	Brundage/Fowler
	1100 cc Sports	O'Shea/Koster
Tulip Rally	1300 cc GT	Amman/Suardi
	1600 cc GT	Andersen/Rottbol-Orum
Mille Miglia	1500 cc Sports	Seidel
	1300 cc GT	von Frankenberg
Le Mans 24-Hours	1500 cc	Polenski/von Frankenberg
	Index	Polenski/von Frankenberg
	1100 cc	Duntov/Veuillet
Rally to the Midnight Sun	1500 cc GT	Borgefors/Gustavson
RAC Tourist Trophy	1500 cc	Shelby/Gregory
	Production Prize	Shelby/Gregory
1956		
Monte Carlo Rally	1300 cc GT	Gacon/Arcan
Lyon-Charbonnieres Rally	2000 cc GT	Gacon/Arcan
	Overall	Gacon/Arcan
Mille Miglia	1300 cc GT	Strahle
	1600 cc GT	Persson/Lundquist
Prix de Paris	2000 cc GT	Storez
Tulip Rally	1600 cc GT	Slotemaker/Beckering
Spa Production Car GP	1500 cc Sports	von Frankenberg
	1600 cc GT	Nathan
Geneva Rally	1600 cc GT	Beyer/Perrot
Nürburg 1,000 Kms	Sports	von Trips/Maglioli
Targa Florio	Overall	Maglioli
	1500 cc Sports	Maglioli
Paris 1,000 Kms	Prod Sports	Goethals/Harris
Reims 12-Hours	1500 cc Sports	von Frankenberg/Storez
Le Mans 24-Hours	1500 cc Sports	von Frankenberg/von Trips
Swiss Mountain GP	Sports	von Hanstein
Berlin GP, AVUS	Sports	von Trips
Nassau Trophy	1600 cc Sports	Miles
1957		
Sebring 12-Hours	Index	Bunker/Wallace
Tulip Rally	1600 cc GT	Gerlach/Brug
Mille Miglia	1500 cc Sports	Maglioli
	1600 cc GT	Strahle/Linge
Spa GP	2600 cc GT	"Max"
	1500 cc Sports	Goethals

EVENT	CLASS	DRIVER/CREW
Nürburgring 1,000 Kms	Sports	Maglioli/Barth
	1600 cc GT	Strahle/Denk
German Rally	2000 cc GT	"Max"/Lissmann
Portuguese GP	1500 cc Sports	de Oliveira
Prix de Paris	1500 cc Sports	Goethals
Le Mans 24-Hours	1500 cc Sports	Hugus/de Beaufort
F2 German GP	Formula 2	Barth
German GP meeting	2000 cc GT	Walter
Gaisberg Hill-Climb	1600 cc GT	Greger
Swiss Mountain GP	2000 cc GT	von Trips
	Special GT	von Hanstein
Watkins Glen races	2000 cc Sports	Holbert
Pomona sports races	Sports	Kunstle
	1500 cc Touring	Bracker
Nassau Trophy	1500 cc Sports	Rodriguez
1958		
Lyon-Charbonnieres Rally	GT	Storez/Buchet
Sebring 12-Hours	1600 cc GT	von Hanstein/Linge
Tulip Rally	1600 cc GT	Schorr/Poll
Rossfeld Hill-Climb	Overall	Greger
	1600 cc GT	Greger
Targa Florio	1500 cc Sports	Behra/Scarlatti
	1600 cc GT	von Hanstein/Pucci
German Rally	1600 cc GT	Walter/Strahle
Nürburg 1,000 Kms	1500 cc Sports	von Frankenberg/de Beaufort/Barth
	1600 cc GT	Strahle/Walter
Mont Ventoux Hill-Climb	Overall	Behra
	1600 cc GT	von Hanstein
Reims 12-Hours	2000 cc GT	von Frankenberg/Storez
Reims GP	Formula 2	Behra
Trento-Bondone Hill-Climb	Overall	von Trips
	2600 cc GT	von Hanstein
Schauinsland Hill-Climb	1600 cc GT	Strahle
German GP meeting	1500 cc Sports	Behra
Gaisberg Hill-Climb	Overall	von Trips
	1600 cc GT	Greger
	1500 cc Sports	von Frankenberg
Swiss Mountain GP	1600 cc GT	Calderari
	1500 cc Sports	Behra
	Special GT	von Hanstein
	2000 cc Sports	Schiller
Coppa InterEuropa	2000 cc GT	von Hanstein
Nassau races	Sports	Rodriguez
1959		
Cape Town Trophy	Formula 2	Fraser Jones
Sebring 12-Hours	2000 cc Sports	von Trips/Bonnier
	1600 cc GT	von Hanstein/de Beaufort
Daytona races	Overall	Von Dory/Mieres
Tulip Rally	1600 cc GT	Gorris/Wiedouw
Prix de Paris	1500 cc Sports	Schell
Spa Grand Prix	2000 cc GT	Walter
Targa Florio	Overall	Barth/Seidel
	2600 cc GT	von Hanstein/Pucci
Nürburg 1,000 Kms	1600 cc GT	Walter/Strahle
	2000 cc Sports	Maglioli/Herrmann
Monza Lottery GP	1600 cc GT	von Hanstein
Mont Ventoux Hill-Climb	Overall	Barth
Trento-Bondone Hill-Climb	Overall	Barth
	2600 cc GT	von Hanstein
Schauinsland Hill-Climb	Championship	Barth
	1600 cc GT	Greger
Gaisberg Hill-Climb	Overall	Vogel
Watkins Glen races	1500 cc Sports	Blanchard
German Rally	1600 cc GT	Debra/Vernaeve
1960		
Buenos Aires 1,000 Kms	1600 cc Sports	Bonnier/Hill
	1600 cc GT	von Hanstein/Bohnen
Lyon-Charbonnieres Rally	Overall	Boutin/Motte
	1600 cc GT	Boutin/Motte
Sebring 12-Hours	1600 cc Sports	Gendebien/Herrmann
	2000 cc GT	Sheppard/Dungan
	Overall	Gendebien/Herrmann
Riverside GP	Production	Barker
Aintree races	Formula 2	Moss
Targa Florio	Overall	Bonnier/Herrmann
	1600 cc Sports	Barth/G. Hill
	2000 cc Sports	Bonnier/Herrmann
Nürburg 1,000 Kms	2000 cc GT	Strahle/Walter
	2000 cc Sports	Bonnier/Gendebien
Spa Grand Prix	Overall	"Braun"
Rouen Grand Prix	2000 cc GT	Koch
Le Mans 24-Hours	1600 cc Sports	Barth/Seidel
	1600 cc GT	Linge/Walter
Norisring races	1600 cc GT	Greger
German GP	Formula 2	Bonnier

EVENT	CLASS	DRIVER/CREW
...wiss Mountain GP	Formula 2	Barth
	2000 cc GT	von Hanstein
...oppa InterEuropa	2000 cc GT	von Hanstein
...aisberg Hill-Climb	Overall	Greger
...Watkins Glen GP	2000 cc Sports	Penske
...oupes de Paris	2000 cc GT	"Schwartz"
...erman Rally	1600 cc GT	Heyse/Schuller
...aris 1,000 Kms	1600 cc GT	von Hanstein/Hill
...outh African GP	Overall	Moss

1961

EVENT	CLASS	DRIVER/CREW
...ebring 12-Hours	Sports	Holbert/Penske
	Index	Holbert/Penske
...arga Florio	Sports	Bonnier/Gurney
...pa Grand Prix	2500 cc GT	Hahnl
...ürburg 1,000 Kms	2000 cc Sports	Linge/Greger
	2000 cc GT	Hahn/Zick
...ouen Grand Prix	2000 cc GT	Monneret
...a Faucille Hill-Climb	Overall	Spychiger
	1600 cc GT	Schiller
...ossfeld Hill-Climb	Overall	Walter
	1600 cc Sports	Walter
...ont Ventoux Hill-Climb	Overall	Walter
...orisring races	Overall	Greger
...rento-Bondone Hill-Climb	Overall	Greger
	2500 cc GT	Gunther
...netterton races	2000 cc GT	Stoop
...chauinsland Hill-Climb	1600 cc Sports	Walter
...erman GP meeting	2000 cc GT	Leinenweber
...wiss Mountain GP	2000 cc GT	Schiller
	1600 cc Sports	Greger
...Watkins Glen GP	Sports	Holbert
...lockenheim 12-Hours	1600 cc GT	Hahnl
...aris 1,000 Kms	1600 cc GT	von Hanstein/Barth
...ome Grand Prix	Formula 1	Baghetti

1962

EVENT	CLASS	DRIVER/CREW
...Monte Carlo Rally	1600 cc GT	Isenbugel/Springer
...yon-Charbonnieres-tuttgart-Solitude Rally	2000 cc GT	Glemser/Wutherich
...ulip Rally	1600 cc GT	Meur/Rousselle
...urban 6-Hours	Overall	Gous/Austin
...arga Florio	1600 cc GT	Herrmann/Linge
	2000 cc Prototype	Bonnier/Vaccarella
...VUS races	1600 cc GT	Koch
...ürburg 1,000 Kms	2000 cc Prototype	G. Hill/Herrmann
	1600 cc GT	Barth/Linge
	2000 cc Sports	Walter/Muller
...aguna Seca races	1500 cc Sports	Masterson
...e Mans 24-Hours	1600 cc	Barth/Herrmann
...orisring races	1600 cc GT	Koch
...rench Grand Prix	Formula 1	Gurney
...rento-Bondone Hill-Climb	2500 cc GT	Gunther
...olitude Grand Prix	Formula 1	Gurney
...chauinsland Hill-Climb	1600 cc GT	Greger
...aytona races	Sports	Ryan
...osport Park races	Sports	Heimrath
...aisberg Hill-Climb	2000 cc Sports	Greger
	1600 cc Sports	Muller
...aris Cups	2000 cc Sports	Fraissinet
...uerto Rico GP	2000 cc Sports	Gurney
...asmanian sports	Overall	Hallam

1963

EVENT	CLASS	DRIVER/CREW
...aytona Challenge Cup	2000 cc GT	von Hanstein
...aytona Continental	2000 cc GT	Bonnier
...yon-Charbonnieres-olitude Rally	2000 cc GT	Buchet/Gauvin
	2700 cc GT	Stoop
...netterton races	2000 cc GT	Holbert/Wester
...ebring 12-Hours	1600 cc GT	Cassel/Sesslar
	1600 cc GT	Humbach/Backer
...ulip Rally	1600 cc GT	
...apanese GP	!000–2000 cc GT	von Hanstein
...arga Florio	Overall	Bonnier/Abate
	Prototypes	Bonnier/Abate
	GT—Overall	Barth/Linge
	2000 cc GT	Barth/Linge
	1600 cc GT	Koch/Schroter
...ancorchamps 500 Kms	1600 cc GT	Stoop
	2000 cc GT	Koch
...ürburg 1,000 Kms	1600 cc GT	Koch/Strahle
	2000 cc GT	Walter/Pon/Barth/Linge
...sfeld Hill-Climb	1600 cc GT	Greger
	2000 cc GT	Barth
	GT—Overall	Barth
...ans 24-Hours	2000 cc	Barth/Linge
...t Ventoux Hill-Climb	Overall	Walter
	2000 cc GT	Muller
...enheim races	2000 cc GT	Linge
	1600 cc GT	Weber
...C Watkins Glen	Overall	Holbert
...paden Rally	GT—Overall	Exner/Wallrebenstein
	1600 cc GT	Exner/Wallrebenstein
	Over 1600 cc GT	Walter/Gastell

EVENT	CLASS	DRIVER/CREW
Trento-Bondone Hill-Climb	Overall	Barth
	GT—Overall	Muller
	1600 cc GT	Mohr
	2500 cc GT	Muller
	Prototypes	Barth
Cesana-Sestriere Hill-Climb	Overall	Barth
	1600 cc GT	Gunther
	2000 cc GT	Muller
Solitude Grand Prix	2500 cc GT	Bonnier
	1600 cc GT	Linge
Schauinsland Hill-Climb	Overall	Barth
	Sports	Barth
	1600 cc GT	Weber
	2000 cc GT	Muller
Gaisberg Hill-Climb	Overall	Barth
	1600 cc GT	Weber
	2000 cc GT	Muller
	Sports	Barth
Geneva Rally	GT—Overall	Walter/Lier

1964

EVENT	CLASS	DRIVER/CREW
Monte Carlo Rally	2000 cc GT	Klass/Wencher
Sebring 12-Hours	Under 2000 cc Prototypes	Cunningham/Underwood
	Under 2000 cc GT	Pon/Buzzetta
Belgian Cup races	Overall	"Elde"
	Sports-Prototype	"Elde'"
	2000 cc GT	"Carlos"
Tulip Rally	2500 cc GT	Crone-Rawe/Crone-Rawe
	1600 cc GT	Gass/Frey
Targa Florio	Overall	Pucci/Davis
	2000 cc GT	Pucci/Davis
	Prototypes	Barth/Maglioli
Munich-Vienna-Budapest Rally	2000 cc GT	Federhofer/Winkler
Spa Grand Prix	2000 cc GT	Barth
Prix de Paris	2000 cc GT	Koch
Semperit Rally	1600 cc GT	Jager/Mossegger
	2000 cc GT	Gass/Sackl
Nürburg 1,000 Kms	2000 cc GT	Pon/Koch
	2000 cc Prototypes	Bonnier/Ginther
Rossfeld Hill-Climb	Overall	Barth
Mont Ventoux Hill-Climb	Overall	Barth
	1600 cc GT	Wambolt
	2000 cc GT	Walter
Le Mans 24-Hours	2000 cc GT	Buchet/Ligier
Mugello race	Overall	Bulgari
Alpine Rally	2500 cc GT	Rey/Hanrioud
Gaisberg Hill-Climb	2000 cc Sports	Barth
	1600 cc GT	Walter
Reims 12-Hours	2000 cc GT	Vianini/Nasif
Norisring races	1600 cc GT	Greger
Trento-Bondone Hill-Climb	Overall	Barth
Luxembourg GP	GT & Prototype	Pon
Cesana-Sestriere Hill-Climb	Overall	Barth
Schauinsland Hill Climb	Overall	Barth
Watkins Glen '500'	E-Prod	Ziereis
Zandvoort races	1600 cc GT	Pon
Coppa InterEuropa	Overall	Slotemaker
Prescott Hill-Climb	2000 cc Sports	Barth
Interlagos 6-Hours	Overall	Landi
Canadian GP	2000 cc	Buzzetta
Paris 1,000 Kms	2000 cc Prototypes	Barth/Davis
Geneva Rally	1600 cc GT	Cuenod/Buel
	2500 cc GT	Meier/Schmalz

1965

EVENT	CLASS	DRIVER/CREW
Monte Carlo Rally	2000 cc GT	Bohringer/Wutherich
Daytona Continental	2000 cc GT	Kolb/Heftler
Stuttgart-Lyon-Charbonnieres Rally	GT	Hanrioud/Rey
Montseny Hill-Climb	Overall	Garcia
	2000 cc GT	Garcia
Heibronner Hill-Climb	Overall	Stommelen
	2000 cc GT	Stommelen
	1600 cc GT	Seidel
Monza 1,000 Kms	2000 cc GT	Pon/Slotemaker
Targa Florio	2000 cc Prototypes	Mitter/Davis
	2000 cc GT	Klass/Pucci
Semperit Rally	2000 cc GT	Wallrabenstein/Herborn
	1600 cc GT	Gass/Bretthauer
Spa 500 Kms	2000 cc GT	Pon
Zandvoort 2-Hours	1600 cc GT	Sailer
Rossfeld Hill-Climb	Overall	Mitter
	2000 cc Sports & PT	Mitter
	2000 cc GT	Muller
Le Mans 24-Hours	2000 cc Prototypes	Linge/Nocker
	Index	Linge/Nocker
	2000 cc GT	Koch/Fischaber
German Rally	2000 cc GT	Wallrabenstein/Herborn
Norisring races	2000 cc Sports & PT	Mitter
	2500 cc GT	Klass
Trento-Bondone Hill-Climb	2500 cc GT	Muller
Solitude Grand Prix	2500 cc GT	Pon
	2000 cc Sports & PT	Mitter

EVENT	CLASS	DRIVER/CREW
Happburg Hill-Climb	2500 cc GT	Stommelen
	1600 cc GT	Seidel
Nürburg Marathon de la Route	GT—Overall	Ising/Degner
Swiss Mountain GP	2000 cc GT	Muller
Zandvoort Trophy	2500 cc GT	Pon
Bridgehampton Double-'500'	2000 cc GT	Wetanson
Gaisberg Hill-Climb	Overall	Weber
Munich-Vienna-Budapest Rally	2000 cc GT	Gass/Bretthauer
	1600 cc GT	Fuss/Wendlinger

1966

EVENT	CLASS	DRIVER/CREW
Daytona 24-Hours	2000 cc Sports	Mitter/Buzzetta
	2000 cc Prototypes	Herrmann/Linge
La Roche Samree Hill-Climb	Overall	Gaban
	2000 cc Sports	Gaban
	2000 cc GT	"Kookie"
Hesse Rally	Overall	Wallrabenstein/Bretthauser
	2000 cc GT	Wallrabenstein/Bretthauser
Sebring 12-Hours	2000 cc Prototypes	Herrmann/Buzzetta/Mitter
	2000 cc Sports	Follmer/Gregg
	2000 cc GT	Ryan/Coleman
S. Australian Hill-Climb	Overall	Hamilton
Stallavena Hill-Climb	Overall	"Noris"
Monza 1,000 Kms	2000 cc Sports	Weber/Neerpasch
Tulip Rally	2500 cc GT	Gass/Bretthauser
	1600 cc GT	Berg/von Moll
Trier airfield races	2000 cc Sports	Schutz
Skarpnack races	2000 cc Sports	Axelsson
Targa Florio	Overall	Mairesse/Muller
	2000 cc Sports	Mairesse/Muller
	1600 cc GT	Tarenghi/Pardi
Cividale-Castelmonte	Overall	"Noris"
La Semois Hill-Climb	Overall	Gaban
Monza races	2000 cc Sports	Vogele
Montseny Hill-Climb	2000 cc GT	Fernandez
Hockenheim '100'	2000 cc Sports	Schutz
	2000 cc GT	Kater
Zandvoort 2-Hours	2000 cc GT	Werlich
Nürburg 1,000 Kms	1600 cc Prototypes	Jost/Dorner
	2000 cc GT	Greger/Auer
	1600 cc GT	Sailer/Lammers
Rossfeld Hill-Climb	Overall	Mitter
	GT—Overall	Mahle
	2000 cc GT	Mahle
Le Mans 24-Hours	Index	Siffert/Davis
	2000 cc Prototypes	Siffert/Davis
	2000 cc Sports	Klass/Stommelen
Mainz airfield races	2000 cc Sports	Mitter
Keimola races	Overall	Wihuri
Mont-Ventoux Hill-Climb	Overall	Mitter
Turkheim Hill-Climb	Overall	Barret
Axamer Hill-Climb	Overall	Lins
Mendel Hill-Climb	Overall	"Noris"
Trento-Bondone Hill-Climb	Overall	Mitter
	2000 cc Sports	Greger
	1600 cc GT	Mahle
Templestowe Hill-Climb	Overall	Hamilton
German Rally	Overall	Klass/Wutherich
Norisring races	Overall	Mitter
Circuit of Mugello	Overall	Koch/Neerpasch
South Carolina USRRC	Overall	Gregg
Schauinsland Hill-Climb	Overall	Mitter
Hockenheim races	Overall	Mitter
AVUS races	2000 cc GT	Pauli/Mahr
Gaisberg Hill-Climb	Overall	Mitter
Elkhart Lake '500'	2000 cc Sports	Buzzetta/Klass
Watkins Glen '500'	Overall	Posey/Caldwell
Alpine Rally	GT—Overall	Klass/Wutherich
	2000 cc GT	Klass/Wutherich
Guadalupe Grand Prix	Overall	von Bayern
Zandvoort races	Overall	Pon
Munich-Vienna-Budapest Rally	2000 cc GT	Gass/Frey
Tirol races	Overall	Mitter
Jarasbei Hill-Climb	Overall	King Hussein
	GT—Overall	King Hussein
Tour of Corsica	2500 cc GT & Sports	Elford/Stone

1967

EVENT	CLASS	DRIVER/CREW
Monte Carlo Rally	GT	Elford/Stone
Daytona 24-Hours	2000 cc Prototypes	Herrmann/Siffert
German Rally	Overall	Elford/Stone
	2000 cc GT	Elford/Stone
Florida 4-Hours	Overall	Mitter/von Wendt
	2000 cc Touring	Mitter/von Wendt
Sebring 12-Hours	2000 cc Touring	Gregg/Posey
	2000 cc Prototypes	Mitter/Patrick
	GT—Overall	Kirby/Johnson
Monza 1,000 Kms	2000 cc Prototypes	Mitter/Rindt
	2000 cc Sports	Schutz/Neerpasch
Tulip Rally	Overall	Elford/Stone
	2000 cc GT	Elford/Stone

EVENT	CLASS	DRIVER/CREW
Spa 1,000 Kms	2000 cc Prototypes	Herrmann/Siffert
Silverstone GP 5 race	Special Touring	Elford
Targa Florio	Overall	Stommelen/Hawkins
	Over 2000 cc Prototypes	Stommelen/Hawkins
	2000 cc Prototypes	Cella/Biscaldi
	GT—Overall	Killy/Cahier
Montseny Hill-Climb	Overall	Mitter
	2000 cc Prototypes	Mitter
	2000 cc Sports	Lins
	GT	Huth
Nürburg 1,000 Kms	2000 cc Prototypes	Schutz/Buzzetta
	Over 2000 cc Prototypes	Mitter/Bianchi
	2000 cc Sports	Dechent/Huhn
	2000 cc GT	Kelleners/Neuhaus
Rossfeld Hill-Climb	Overall	Stommelen
	2000 cc Sports	Greger
	2000 cc GT	Fischaber
	2000 cc Touring	Dau
Le Mans 24-Hours	Sports—Overall	Elford/Pon
	2000 cc GT	Buchet/Linge
	2000 cc Prototypes	Siffert/Herrmann
Geneva Rally	Overall	Elford/Stone
	2000 cc GT	Elford/Stone
	1600 cc Touring	Zasada/Dobrzanski
Reims 12-Hours	2000 cc Prototypes	Spoerry/Steinemann
	2000 cc Sports	Buchet/Herrmann
	2000 cc GT	Garant/Rey
Mont Ventoux Hill-Climb	Overall	Stommelen
	Sports—Overall	Lins
	GT—Overall	Hanrioud
Trento-Bondone Hill-Climb	Overall	Mitter
	2000 cc Sports	Lins
	2000 cc GT	Fischaber
	2000 cc Touring	Gerin
Cesana-Sestriere Hill-Climb	Overall	Stommelen
	2000 cc Sports	Greger
	2000 cc GT	Fischaber
	2000 cc Touring	Nyffeler
Francorchamps 24-Hours	Overall	Gaban/"Pedro"
Nürburgring 12-Hours	GT	Falz/Pilz
	2000 cc Touring	Bergmann/Mohr
Circuit of Mugello	Overall	Mitter
	2000 cc Sports	Greger
	2000 cc GT	Fischaber
	2000 cc Touring	Zarges
BOAC '500'	Over 2000 cc Prototypes	Siffert/McLaren
	2000 cc Sports	Dean/Pon
Polish Rally	Overall	Zasada/Zasada
Nürburg Marathon de la Route	Overall	Herrmann/Neerpasch Elford
Zandvoort races	Overall	Pon
Gaisberg Hill-Climb	Overall	Stommelen
	2000 cc Sports	Lins
Hockenheim races	Prototypes	Walter
	2000 cc Sports	Werlich
	2000 cc GT	Ernst
Aspern airfield races	2000 cc Prototypes	Schutz
Laguna Seca races	Overall	Patrick
Paris 1,000 Kms	GT—Overall	Buchet/Linge
Argentine Road Race	Overall	Zasada
	2000 cc Touring	Zasada
Marlboro '300'	Overall	Everett/Titus
Tour of Corsica	GT—Overall	Hanrioud/Constantini

1968

EVENT	CLASS	DRIVER/CREW
Swedish Rally	Overall	Waldegard/Helmer
Monte Carlo Rally	Overall	Elford/Stone
	GT	Elford/Stone
Daytona 24-Hours	Overall and Prototypes	Elford/Neerpasch/ Stommelen/Siffert/ Herrmann
	Touring	Gregg/Axelsson
	GT	Hanrioud/Garant
Sebring 12-Hours	Overall	Siffert/Herrmann
Monza 4-Hours	Overall	Kelleners/Kremer
East German Rally	Overall	Toivonen/Vihervaara
BOAC '500'	2000 cc Group 6	Spoerry/Steinemann
	3000 cc Group 6	Mitter/Scarfiotti
German Rally	Overall	Toivonen/Kolari
Monza 1,000 Kms	GT	Glemser/Kelleners
Targa Florio	Overall	Elford/Maglioli
	Sports	von Wendt/Kaussen
	GT	Haldi/Greub
Montseny Hill-Climb	Overall	Mitter
Nürburg 1,000 Kms	Overall	Siffert/Elford
	Group 3	Greger/Huth
Rossfeld Hill-Climb	Overall	Mitter
Francorchamps 1,000 Kms	Group 6	Mitter/Schlesser
	Group 3	Kelleners/Glemser
	2000 cc Group 4	Bradley/Lambert
RAC Tourist Trophy	2000 cc Group 4	Bradley
Gulf London Rally	Overall	Andersson/Svedberg
Cesana-Sestriere Hill-Climb	Overall	Mitter
Freiburg Hill-Climb	Overall	Mitter

This list covers purely outright and class wins, and only the more notable ones at that.